Everyday We Praise You

"Alleluia. The Lord our powerful God is King; let us rejoice, sing praise, and give him glory. Alleluia."

EVERY DAY
WE PRAISE YOU

PRAYERS, READINGS, and DEVOTIONS
FOR THE YEAR

Including Morning and Evening Prayer
from the "Liturgy of the Hours"
(1st Week)

Edited by

Victor Hoagland, C.P.

Maureen Skelly, S.C.

CATHOLIC BOOK PUBLISHING CO.
NEW YORK

NIHIL OBSTAT: Daniel V. Flynn, J.C.D.
Censor Librorum

IMPRIMATUR: Joseph T. O'Keefe
Vicar General, Archdiocese of New York

(T-315)

CONTENTS

INTRODUCTION

"Lord, teach us to pray."

LIKE the disciples of Jesus long ago, we wish in our day to know how to pray. This prayer book seeks to provide from the treasures of the Church's liturgy and devotions some ways for men and women to pray today. It can be used by individuals praying alone or with others.

You will find here the complete Morning and Evening Prayer from the first week of the Liturgy of the Hours, with some aids for community celebration of these prayers, if this be desired. The Church warmly recommends these daily prayers to her people as a way of uniting themselves to the prayer of Jesus Christ. You may wish to say them at the beginning and end of your day. They would be fitting prayers too for parish communities or groups on retreat engaged in days of prayer.

In order to appreciate the prayer of the hours better, particularly the psalms, short commentaries have been added to introduce them. Music has also been provided for celebrating the prayer in common. If you are going to pray the hours in common, the suggestions made later on in this introduction may prove helpful.

The mysteries of Christ offer continual nourishment for Christian prayer. During the year you may wish to use the readings and prayers in this book to meditate on the great Christian mysteries that occur during the Advent, Lent and Easter seasons. Besides passages of scripture, selections from the writings and prayers of the saints and spiritual writers are included to aid your spiritual reflection.

The prayers and readings for Mass are already available in hand missals. Worship of the Eucharist outside of Mass has not been as well provided for. In this book you will find readings, prayers and reflections that may be used for services of Benediction during the year, or for private prayer, or for those times when Communion is received outside of Mass. If you are homebound and receive the Holy Eucharist outside Mass you may find helpful the prayers and readings on the Eucharist presented here.

The new Rite of Penance is provided to enable you to celebrate this sacrament of reconciliation and peace.

Besides liturgical prayer, various devotions have nourished the Christian spirit throughout the ages. An arrangement of the Stations of the Cross, which can be used individually or communally, is presented here. Other traditional prayers, cherished by Christians, have been collected for your devotion.

A general view of methods and techniques of prayer can be found on p. 143. A careful reading of this section may be a good introduction to all the different forms of prayer this book offers you.

SUGGESTIONS FOR PRAYING
IN COMMON

PREPARING for prayer in common is a vital step to praying well. Generally, our minds and bodies need necessary time and appropriate space to pray. Before beginning common prayer, therefore, it would be well to provide the group with a few minutes of silence or the opportunity to listen to a short piece of quiet music, preferably without words, in order to gather its attention for what is before it. A certain wholeheartedness is necessary for prayer, and a scattered mind cannot give itself wholly. Time to become just attentive is never wasted. This is all the more necessary when a group is engaged in some previous activity that is particularly engrossing.

The place chosen for group prayer should be conducive to praying together. The room should be adequate to the size of the group. Often a small group can feel lost or out-of-touch in a large or inadequately arranged space. A special place, used consistently and visually appropriate, can diminish distractions and lead to prayerful participation.

The pace of prayer is important. Since the predominant tendency is to rush in group prayer, great care should be taken to ensure an unhurried pace, to provide moments of relaxed silence, and to allow for savoring the Word of God. Moments of silence can be suitably placed after each

psalm and after the reading as an aid to hearing
God's word and personally assimilating its meaning.

The leader of prayer, the readers, and those
who lead the music have a particular role in es-
tablishing a good pace for celebration.

A time of silence at the end of the prayer
would also be appropriate for that joyful contemplation which is the final stage of prayer itself.

Music

Music settings have been provided for canticles, antiphons and psalms. These are simple to
sing. In morning and evening prayer, the antiphons for the psalms may be sung by the community or an individual at the beginning of the
psalm and after every few verses or strophes, as
seems fit. The nature of the psalm as a prayer of
an individual or of the community will help determine whether it be recited by an individual or
by the community.

The antiphon sets the mood for the psalm; the
psalm tones are taken from notes already contained in the antiphon.

The suggested psalm tones may be used either
alone or in combination. Example:

When Israel came forth from Egypt,
Jacob's sons from an alien people,
Tone 1/or Tone 2
Judah became the Lord's temple,
Israel became his kingdom.
Tone 1 and Tone 2

When there are three verses, the last part of the tone is repeated.

Other hymns and antiphons better known to the group can be substituted for those offered here.

The group's ability to sing, the nature of the day and the celebration will help determine how much music will be used. Not all has to be sung; not all has to be recited.

PRINCIPAL CELEBRATIONS OF LITURGICAL YEAR

Year	Lectionary Sunday Cycle	Ash Wednes.	Easter	Ascension	Pentecost	Corpus Christi	First Sun. of Advent
1978	A	8 Feb.	26 Mar.	4 May	14 May	25 May	3 Dec.
1979	B	28 Feb.	15 Apr.	24 May	3 June	14 June	2 Dec.
1980	C	20 Feb.	6 Apr.	15 May	25 May	5 June	30 Nov.
1981	A	4 Mar.	19 Apr.	28 May	7 June	18 June	29 Nov.
1982	B	24 Feb.	11 Apr.	20 May	30 May	10 June	28 Nov.
1983	C	16 Feb.	3 Apr.	12 May	22 May	2 June	27 Nov.
1984	A	7 Mar.	22 Apr.	31 May	10 June	21 June	2 Dec.
1985	B	20 Feb.	7 Apr.	16 May	26 May	6 June	1 Dec.
1986	C	12 Feb.	30 Mar.	8 May	18 May	29 May	30 Nov.
1987	A	4 Mar.	19 Apr.	28 May	7 June	18 June	29 Nov.
1988	B	17 Feb.	3 Apr.	12 May	22 May	2 June	27 Nov.
1989	C	8 Feb.	26 Mar.	4 May	14 May	25 May	3 Dec.
1990	A	28 Feb.	15 Apr.	24 May	3 June	14 June	2 Dec.
1991	B	13 Feb.	31 Mar.	9 May	19 May	30 May	1 Dec.
1992	C	4 Mar.	19 Apr.	28 May	7 June	18 June	29 Nov.
1993	A	24 Feb.	11 Apr.	20 May	30 May	10 June	28 Nov.
1994	B	16 Feb.	3 Apr.	12 May	22 May	2 June	27 Nov.
1995	C	1 Mar.	16 Apr.	25 May	4 June	15 June	3 Dec.
1996	A	21 Feb.	7 Apr.	16 May	26 May	6 June	1 Dec.
1997	B	12 Feb.	30 Mar.	8 May	18 May	29 May	30 Nov.
1998	C	25 Feb.	12 Apr.	21 May	31 May	11 June	29 Nov.
1999	A	17 Feb.	4 Apr.	13 May	23 May	3 June	28 Nov.

THE PSALTER

(1st Week)

The Psalms are the prayer of God's assembly, the public prayer par excellence of the people of God. They recall to mind the truths revealed by God to the chosen people; they keep repeating and fostering the hope of the promised Redeemer, and they show forth in splendid light the prophesied glory of Jesus Christ.

In a similar way they express the joy, the bitterness, the hope and fear of our hearts and our desire of loving God and hoping in him alone, and our mystic ascent to divine tabernacles.

SUNDAY EVENING I

Reflection

PSALM 141 is one of the Church's traditional evening prayers. It is a prayer we can all say, Saint Augustine observes, for it is a prayer of the body of Christ, the Church. Sometimes Christ prays in his Church as she is in anguish; sometimes he prays in us as we rejoice. But we are never alone in prayer. Christ has made us his own, and so we share in his life, his merits, and his prayer.

The incense we offer, the evening oblation we make is the passion of the Lord. "When day was fading into evening, the Lord laid down his life on the cross," Saint Augustine says; "in his resurrection he made this evening sacrifice a morning offering."

As this day ends, our own offering to God is made with that of Christ's. His merits and prayers make what we do acceptable before God, the Father. Our lives this day are brought to the Father through him.

So it is that "at Jesus' name every knee must bend in the heavens, on the earth, and under the earth, and every tongue proclaim to the glory of God the Father: Jesus Christ is Lord!"

EVENING PRAYER I

GOD, come to my assistance.
— Lord, make haste to help me.
Glory to the Father, and to the Son, and to the
   Holy Spirit:
— as it was in the beginning, is now, and will be
   for ever. Amen. Alleluia.

Hymn no. 24 or see Guide, 348.

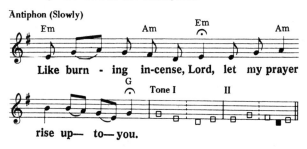

Antiphon (Slowly)

Like burn - ing in-cense, Lord, let my prayer
rise up— to— you.

Psalm 141:1-9

A prayer when in danger

*An angel stood before the face of God, thurible
in hand. The fragrant incense soaring aloft was
the prayer of God's people on earth (Revelation
8:4).*

I HAVE called to you, Lord; hasten to help
   me!
Hear my voice when I cry to you.
Let my prayer arise before you like incense,
the raising of my hands like an evening oblation.

Set, O Lord, a guard over my mouth;

keep watch at the door of my lips!
Do not turn my heart to things that are
    wrong,
to evil deeds with men who are sinners.

Never allow me to share in their feasting.
If a good man strikes or reproves me it is
    kindness;
but let the oil of the wicked not anoint my
    head.
Let my prayer be ever against their malice.

Their princes were thrown down by the side
    of the rock:
then they understood that my words were
    kind.
As a millstone is shattered to pieces on the
    ground,
so their bones were strewn at the mouth of
    the grave.

To you, Lord God, my eyes are turned:
in you I take refuge; spare my soul!
From the trap they have laid for me keep me
    safe:
keep me from the snares of those who do
    evil.

Glory to the Father, and to the Son, and to the
    Holy Spirit:
as it was in the beginning, is now, and will be
    for ever. Amen.

Psalm-prayer
    Lord, from the rising of the sun to its setting
your name is worthy of all praise. Let our prayer
come like incense before you. May the lifting up

of our hands be as an evening sacrifice acceptable to you, Lord our God.

Antiphon

You are my ref-uge, Lord; you are all that

I de-sire—— in life.

Psalm 142

You, Lord, are my refuge

*What is written in this psalm was fulfilled in
our Lord's passion* (Saint Hilary).

WITH all my voice I cry to the Lord,
    with all my voice I entreat the Lord.
I pour out my trouble before him;
I tell him all my distress
while my spirit faints within me.
But you, O Lord, know my path.

On the way where I shall walk
they have hidden a snare to entrap me.
Look on my right and see:
there is not one who takes my part.
I have no means of escape,
not one who cares for my soul.

I cry to you, O Lord.
I have said: "You are my refuge,
all I have left in the land of the living."
Listen then to my cry
for I am in the depths of distress.

Rescue me from those who pursue me
for they are stronger than I.
Bring my soul out of this prison
and then I shall praise your name.
Around me the just will assemble
because of your goodness to me.

Glory to the Father, and to the Son, and to the
Holy Spirit:
as it was in the beginning, is now, and will be
for ever. Amen.

Psalm-prayer

Lord, we humbly ask for your goodness. May
you help us to hope in you, and give us a share
with your chosen ones in the land of the living.

Canticle Antiphon

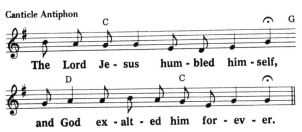

The Lord Je - sus hum - bled him - self,

and God ex - alt - ed him for - ev - er.

Canticle: Philippians 2:6-11
Christ, God's holy servant

THOUGH he was in the form of God,
Jesus did not deem equality with God
something to be grasped at.

Rather, he emptied himself
and took the form of a slave,
being born in the likeness of men.

He was known to be of human estate,
and it was thus that he humbled himself,
obediently accepting even death,
death of a cross!

Because of this,
God highly exalted him
and bestowed on him the name
above every other name,

So that at Jesus' name
every knee must bend
in the heavens, on the earth,
and under the earth,
and every tongue proclaim
to the glory of God the Father:
JESUS CHRIST IS LORD!

Glory to the Father, and to the Son, and to the
    Holy Spirit:
as it was in the beginning, is now, and will be
    for ever. Amen.

Reading

Romans 11:33-36

HOW deep are the riches and the wisdom and
the   knowledge of God! How inscrutable his
judgments, how unsearchable his ways! For
"who has known the mind of the Lord? Or who
has been his counselor? Who has given him
anything so as to deserve return?" For from him
and through him and for him all things are. To
him be glory forever. Amen.

Responsory

Our hearts are filled with wonder, as we contem-
plate your works, O Lord.
—Our hearts are filled with wonder, as we con-
template your works, O Lord.
We praise the wisdom which wrought them all,
—as we contemplate your works, O Lord
Glory to the Father . . .
—Our hearts are . . .

Canticle of Mary

Ant.   My spirit rejoices in God my Savior.*

(Turn to p. 131)

Intercessions

WE GIVE glory to the one God—Father, Son
and Holy Spirit—and in our weakness we
pray:
Lord, be with your people.
Holy Lord, Father all-powerful, let justice spring
up on the earth,
—then your people will dwell in the beauty of
peace.
Let every nation come into your kingdom,
—so that all peoples will be saved.
Let married couples live in your peace,
—and grow in mutual love.
Reward all who have done good to us, Lord,
—and grant them eternal life.
Look with compassion on victims of hatred and
war,
—grant them heavenly peace.

Our Father . . .
* Proper antiphon for Tues, Week I.

Prayer

(16th Sun. Ord. Time)

FATHER,
let the gift of your life
continue to grow in us,
drawing us from death to faith, hope, and love.
Keep us alive in Christ Jesus.
Keep us watchful in prayer
and true to his teaching
till your glory is revealed in us.

Grant this through Christ our Lord.

(Selected concluding prayers for seasons and feasts, pp. 132-141)

(Dismissal, p. 141)

SUNDAY MORNING

Reflection

*The prayers for morning and evening begin
with some verses from the psalms:*

Lord, open my lips.
— And my mouth will proclaim your praise.
God, come to my assistance.
— Lord, make haste to help me.

*Prayer is a gift—God's gift—these opening
verses say. Unless he opens our lips and comes
to our assistance, we cannot pray.*

*"Ask, and you will receive. Seek, and you will
find. Knock, and it will be opened to you"* (Matthew 7:7).

*If we come to prayer like beggars—thirsty,
hungry and poor—then God will spread his gifts
before us. If we come before him forgetful of
ourselves, open and expectant, then he will open
our eyes to the wonders of life.*

*Unless God helps us, we may settle down like
the Pharisee, congratulating ourselves on our
pocketful of small achievements* (Luke 18:9ff), *or
like the rich fool, mistaking the few barns we
possess for the world. "God, come to my assistance." "Lord, open my lips."*

The Canticle of Daniel and Psalm 149 add the song of all creation to our own limited song. United with everything on earth as well as with the saints in heaven, we praise God through Jesus Christ, from whom all life comes.

MORNING PRAYER

LORD, open my lips.
   — And my mouth will proclaim your praise.

Glory to, etc.:   — as it was, etc.

Ant.   Come, let us sing to the Lord, and shout with joy to the Rock who saves us, alleluia.

Invitatory psalm, p. 128.
Hymn no. 16 or see Guide, p. 348.

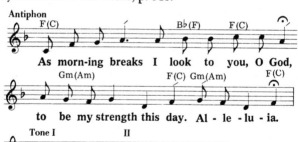

Antiphon

As morn-ing breaks I look to you, O God, to be my strength this day. Al - le - lu - ia.

Tone I   II

Psalm 63:2-9

A soul thirsting for God

Whoever has left the darkness of sin, yearns for God.

O GOD, you are my God for you I long;
for you my soul is thirsting.

My body pines for you
like a dry, weary land without water.
So I gaze on you in the sanctuary
to see your strength and your glory.

For your love is better than life,
my lips will speak your praise.
So I will bless you all my life,
in your name I will lift up my hands.
My soul shall be filled as with a banquet,
my mouth shall praise you with joy.

On my bed I remember you.
On you I muse through the night
for you have been my help;
in the shadow of your wings I rejoice.
My soul clings to you;
your right hand holds me fast.

Glory to the Father, and to the Son, and to the
  Holy Spirit:
as it was in the beginning, is now, and will be
  for ever. Amen.

Psalm-prayer

Father, creator of unfailing light, give that
same light to those who call to you. May our lips
praise you; our lives proclaim your goodness;
our work give you honor, and our voices celebrate you for ever.

Canticle

From the midst   of the flames the three young men

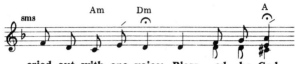

cried out with one voice: Bless - ed   be God,

Al - le - lu - ia.

Canticle: Daniel 3:57-88, 56
Let all creatures praise the Lord

All you servants of the Lord, sing praise to him
(Revelation 19:5).

BLESS the Lord, all you works of the Lord.
Praise and exalt him above all forever.
Angels of the Lord, bless the Lord.
You heavens, bless the Lord.
All you waters above the heavens, bless the Lord.
All you hosts of the Lord, bless the Lord.
Sun and moon, bless the Lord.
Stars of heaven, bless the Lord.

Every shower and dew, bless the Lord.
All you winds, bless the Lord.
Fire and heat, bless the Lord.
Cold and chill, bless the Lord.
Dew and rain, bless the Lord.
Frost and chill, bless the Lord.
Ice and snow, bless the Lord.
Nights and days, bless the Lord.
Light and darkness, bless the Lord.
Lightnings and clouds, bless the Lord.

Let the earth bless the Lord.
Praise and exalt him above all forever.
Mountains and hills, bless the Lord.
Everything growing from the earth, bless the Lord.
You springs, bless the Lord.
Seas and rivers, bless the Lord.
You dolphins and all water creatures, bless the Lord.
All you birds of the air, bless the Lord.
All you beasts, wild and tame, bless the Lord.
You sons of men, bless the Lord.

O Israel, bless the Lord.
Praise and exalt him above all forever.
Priests of the Lord, bless the Lord
Servants of the Lord, bless the Lord.
Spirits and souls of the just, bless the Lord.
Holy men of humble heart, bless the Lord.
Hananiah, Azariah, Mishael, bless the Lord.
Praise and exalt him above all forever.

Let us bless the Father, and the Son, and the Holy Spirit.
Let us praise and exalt him above all forever.
Blessed are you, Lord, in the firmament of heaven.
Praiseworthy and glorious and exalted above all forever.

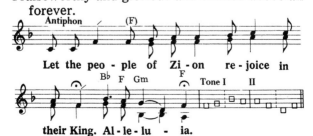

Let the people of Zion rejoice in their King. Alleluia.

Psalm 149

The joy of God's holy people

Let the sons of the Church, the children of the new people, rejoice in Christ, their King (Hesychius).

SING a new song to the Lord,
his praise in the assembly of the faithful.
Let Israel rejoice in its maker,
let Zion's sons exult in their king.
Let them praise his name with dancing
and make music with timbrel and harp.

For the Lord takes delight in his people.
He crowns the poor with salvation.
Let the faithful rejoice in their glory,
shout for joy and take their rest.
Let the praise of God be on their lips
and a two-edged sword in their hand,

to deal out vengeance to the nations
and punishment on all the peoples;
to bind their kings in chains
and their nobles in fetters of iron;
to carry out the sentence pre-ordained;
this honor is for all his faithful.

Glory to the Father, and to the Son, and to the
    Holy Spirit:
as it was in the beginning, is now, and will be
    for ever. Amen.

Psalm-prayer

Let Israel rejoice in you, Lord, and acknowledge you as creator and redeemer. We put our trust in your faithfulness and proclaim the wonderful truths of salvation. May your loving kindness embrace us now and for ever.

Reading

Revelations 7:9-12

AFTER this I saw before me a huge crowd which no one could count from every nation and race, people and tongue. They stood before the throne and the Lamb, dressed in long white robes and holding palm branches in their hands. They cried out in a loud voice, "Salvation is from our God, who is seated on the throne, and from the Lamb!" All the angels who were standing around the throne and the elders and the four living creatures fell down before the throne to worship God. They said: "Amen! Praise and glory, wisdom and thanksgiving and honor, power and might, to our God forever and ever. Amen!"

Responsory

Christ, Son of the living God, have mercy on us.
— Christ, Son of the living God, have mercy on us.
You are seated at the right hand of the Father,
— have mercy on us.
Glory to the Father . . .
— Christ, Son of . . .

Canticle of Zechariah

Ant. Lord, guide our feet into the way of peace*

(Turn to p. 130)

* Proper antiphon for Saturday, Week IV.

Intercessions

CHRIST is the sun that never sets, the true
light that shines on every man. Let us call
out to him in praise:
Lord, you are our life and our salvation.
Creator of the stars, we thank you for your gift,
the first rays of the dawn,
—and we commemorate your resurrection.
May your Holy Spirit teach us to do your will
today,
—and may your Wisdom guide us always.
Each Sunday give us the joy of gathering as your
people,
—around the table of your Word and your Body.
From our hearts we thank you,
—for your countless blessings.

Our Father . . .

Prayer　(18th Sun. Ord. Time)

GOD our Father,
gifts without measure flow from your goodness
to bring us your peace.
Our life is your gift.
Guide our life's journey,
for only your love makes us whole.
Keep us strong in your love.

We ask this through Christ our Lord.

(Selected concluding prayers for seasons and feasts, pp. 132-141)

(Turn to p. 141)

SUNDAY EVENING II
Reflection

EVERY Sunday we celebrate the Resurrection of Christ. Not only did Jesus rise from the dead but he ascended to his heavenly Father, who gave him all power in heaven and on earth.

In Psalm 110, a psalm originally celebrating the day an ancient Israelite king was enthroned amid the joy of his people, we express our faith in the Resurrection of Jesus and his kingship. We celebrate the homecoming of Christ, our Lord.

Before all creation, the Father proclaims the rule of his Son. Like a warrior who has earned his victory, Jesus Christ holds in his hands our yesterdays, todays, and tomorrows. His power flows surely and unceasingly through all time and space.

"A priest, like Melchizedek of old," Jesus Christ offers to his Father a world which is dear to him. A compassionate priest, he knows the sufferings and aspirations of humanity.

A homecoming as well as an enthronement is described in Psalm 110. Can we not know in this psalm the Father's touching, welcoming embrace of his Son, and his ready acceptance of all that is human through his Son's humanity? Can we not

31

see his eyes softening gently at the sight of his wounds? Can God be unmindful of any human grief and suffering since he has tasted it so deeply in the sufferings of Christ?

An ancient people once sang Psalm 110 rejoicing on the day of their king's enthronement. Today we rejoice knowing that the reign of Jesus Christ will never end.

Our union with him is described in Psalm 114 and the Canticle from Revelation. We are like Israel: come forth from Egypt. The power of Christ redeems us.

The day of Christ's enthronement is also "the wedding day of the Lamb." All of us, "great and small," are espoused to him who, from his own riches, clothes us in the fine apparel of his grace.

EVENING PRAYER

God, come to my assistance.
— Lord make haste to help me.
Glory to the Father, and to the Son, and to the Holy Spirit:
— as it was in the beginning, is now, and will be for ever. Amen. Alleluia.

Hymn no. 12 or see Guide, 348.

Antiphon

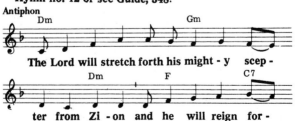

The Lord will stretch forth his might-y scep-ter from Zi-on and he will reign for-

ev - er. Al - le - lu - ia.

Psalm 110:1-5, 7

The Messiah, king and priest

Christ's reign will last until all his enemies are made subject to him (1 Corinthians 15:25).

THE Lord's revelation to my Master:
  "Sit on my right:
your foes I will put beneath your feet."

The Lord will wield from Zion
your scepter of power:
rule in the midst of all your foes.

A prince from the day of your birth
on the holy mountains;
from the womb before the dawn I begot you.

The Lord has sworn an oath he will not
    change.
"You are a priest for ever,
a priest like Melchizedek of old."

The Master standing at your right hand
will shatter kings in the day of his great
    wrath.

He shall drink from the stream by the way-
    side
and therefore he shall lift up his head.

Glory to the Father, and to the Son, and to the
 Holy Spirit:
as it was in the beginning, is now, and will be
 for ever. Amen.

Psalm-prayer

Father, we ask you to give us victory and
peace. In Jesus Christ, our Lord and King, we
are already seated at your right hand. We look
forward to praising you in the fellowship of all
your saints in our heavenly homeland.

Antiphon

The earth is shak-en to its depths be-fore

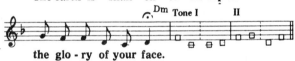

the glo-ry of your face.

Psalm 114

The Israelites are delivered from the bondage of Egypt

*You too left Egypt when, at baptism, you re-
nounced that world which is at enmity with God
(Saint Augustine).*

WHEN Israel came forth from Egypt,
 Jacob's sons from an alien people,
Judah became the Lord's temple,
Israel became his kingdom.

The sea fled at the sight:
the Jordan turned back on its course,

the mountains leapt like rams
and the hills like yearling sheep.

Why was it, sea, that you fled,
that you turned back, Jordan, on your course?
Mountains, that you leapt like rams,
hills, like yearling sheep?

Tremble, O earth, before the Lord,
in the presence of the God of Jacob,
who turns the rock into a pool
and flint into a spring of water.

Glory to the Father, and to the Son, and to the
   Holy Spirit:
as it was in the beginning, is now, and will be
   for ever. Amen.

Psalm-prayer

Almighty God, ever-living mystery of unity
and Trinity, you gave life to the new Israel by
birth from water and the Spirit, and made it a
chosen race, a royal priesthood, a people set apart
as your eternal possession. May all those you
have called to walk in the splendor of the new
light render you fitting service and adoration.

Canticle

All power is yours. Lord God, our migh-ty King. Al - le - lu - ia

(Music for Canticle, p. 366)

Canticle: See Revelation 19:1-7
The wedding of the Lamb

A LLELUIA.
Salvation, glory, and power to our God:
(℟. Alleluia.)
his judgments are honest and true.
℟. Alleluia (alleluia).

Alleluia.
Sing praise to our God, all you his servants,
(℟. Alleluia.)
all who worship him reverently, great and
small.
℟. Alleluia (alleluia).

Alleluia.
The Lord our all-powerful God is King;
(℟. Alleluia.)
let us rejoice, sing praise, and give him glory.
℟. Alleluia (alleluia).

Alleluia.
The wedding feast of the Lamb has begun,
(℟. Alleluia.)
and his bride is prepared to welcome him.
℟. Alleluia (alleluia).

Glory to the Father, and to the Son, and to the
Holy Spirit:
as it was in the beginning, is now, and will be
for ever. Amen.

Reading

2 Corinthians 1:3-4

P RAISED be God, the Father of our Lord Jesus
Christ, the Father of mercies and the God

of all consolation! He comforts us in all our afflictions and thus enables us to comfort those who are in trouble, with the same consolation we have received from him.

Responsory

The whole creation proclaims the greatness of
    your glory.
—The whole creation proclaims the greatness
    of your glory.
Eternal ages praise
—the greatness of your glory.
Glory to the Father . . .
—The whole creation . . .

Canticle of Mary

Ant.   My spirit rejoices in God my Savior.*

(Turn to p. 131)

Intercessions

CHRIST the Lord is our head; we are his members. In joy let us call out to him:
    Lord, may your kingdom come.
Christ our Savior, make your Church a more vivid
    symbol of the unity of all mankind,
—make it more effectively the sacrament of salvation for all peoples.
Through your presence, guide the college of bishops in union with the Pope,
—give them the gifts of unity, love and peace.
Bind all Christians more closely to yourself; their
    divine Head,
—lead them to proclaim your kingdom by the
    witness of their lives.

* Proper antiphon for Tues., Week I.

Grant peace to the world,
— let every land flourish in justice and security.
Grant to the dead the glory of resurrection,
— and give us a share in their happiness.

Our Father , . .

Prayer
(8th Sun. Ord. Time)

FATHER in heaven,
  form in us the likeness of your Son
and deepen his life within us.
Send us as witnesses of gospel joy
into a world of fragile peace and broken
  promises.
Touch the hearts of all men with your love
that they in turn may love one another.

We ask this through Christ our Lord.

(Selected concluding prayers for seasons and feasts, pp. 132-141)

(Turn to p. 141)

MONDAY MORNING

Reflection

"**A** GOOD man is always a beginner," wrote the Roman writer, Martial.

Morning prayer can be a good beginning for the day that is ours today.

"We pray in the morning," says the 4th century bishop, Saint Basil, in one of his writings, "so that the first stirrings of our mind and will may be consecrated to God and that we may take nothing in hand until we have been gladdened by the thought of God." He then adds a verse from Psalm 5: "It is you whom I invoke, O Lord. In the morning you hear me."

Yes, we should begin our life today nourished by faith, hope and love. May our hands take up the new work before us and continue what we have begun. May we complete what God gives us to do.

This morning's psalms, prayers and reading offer us perspective and motivation for the day before us. Whether the circumstances of life are stormy or quiet, may his will be done.

We must never grow weary of doing what is right.

MORNING PRAYER

LORD, open my lips.
   —And my mouth will proclaim your praise.

Glory to, etc.:   — as it was, etc.

Ant.   Let us approach the Lord with praise and
       thanksgiving.

Invitatory psalm, p. 128.
Hymn no. 15 or see Guide, 348.

Antiphon

I lift up my heart to you, O Lord, and you will

hear my morn-ing prayer.

Psalm 5:2-10, 12-13

A morning prayer asking for help

*Those who welcome the Word as the guest of
their hearts will have abiding joy.*

TO MY words give ear, O Lord,
   give heed to my groaning.
Attend to the sound of my cries,
my King and my God.

It is you whom I invoke, O Lord.
In the morning you hear me;
in the morning I offer you my prayer,
watching and waiting.

You are no God who loves evil;
no sinner is your guest.
The boastful shall not stand their ground
before your face.

You hate all who do evil:
you destroy all who lie.
The deceitful and bloodthirsty man
the Lord detests.

But I through the greatness of your love
have access to your house.
I bow down before your holy temple,
filled with awe.

Lead me, Lord, in your justice,
because of those who lie in wait;
make clear your way before me.

No truth can be found in their mouths,
their heart is all mischief,
their throat a wide-open grave,
all honey their speech.

All those you protect shall be glad
and ring out their joy.
You shelter them, in you they rejoice,
those who love your name.

It is you who bless the just man, Lord:
you surround him with favor as with a shield.

Glory to the Father, and to the Son, and to the
Holy Spirit:

as it was in the beginning, is now, and will be
for ever. Amen.

Psalm-prayer

Lord, all justice and all goodness come from
you; you hate evil and abhor lies. Lead us, your
servants, in the path of your justice, so that all
who hope in you may rejoice with the Church
and in Christ.

Antiphon

We praise your glo - ri-ous name, O Lord, our God.

Canticle: 1 Chronicles 29:10-13

Glory and honor are due to God alone

*Blessed be the God and Father of our Lord Jesus
Christ* (Ephesians 1:3).

BLESSED may you be, O Lord,
    God of Israel our father,
from eternity to eternity.

Yours, O Lord, are grandeur and power,
majesty, splendor, and glory.

For all in heaven and on earth is yours;
yours, O Lord, is the sovereignty:
you are exalted as head over all.

Riches and honor are from you,
and you have dominion over all.
In your hands are power and might;
    it is yours to give grandeur and strength to
        all.

Therefore, our God, we give you thanks
and we praise the majesty of your name.

Glory to the Father, and to the Son, and to the
   Holy Spirit:
as it was in the beginning, is now, and will be
   for ever. Amen.

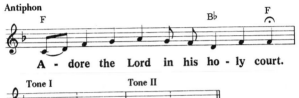

Antiphon

A - dore the Lord in his ho - ly court.

Tone I   Tone II

Psalm 29

A tribute of praise to the Word of God

*The Father's voice proclaimed: "This is my be-
loved Son" (Matthew 3:17).*

O GIVE the Lord, you sons of God,
   give the Lord glory and power;
give the Lord the glory of his name.
Adore the Lord in his holy court.

The Lord's voice resounding on the waters,
the Lord on the immensity of waters;
the voice of the Lord, full of power,
the voice of the Lord, full of splendor.

The Lord's voice shattering the cedars,
the Lord shatters the cedars of Lebanon;
he makes Lebanon leap like a calf
and Sirion like a young wild-ox.

The Lord's voice flashes flames of fire.
The Lord's voice shaking the wilderness,
the Lord shakes the wilderness of Kadesh;
the Lord's voice rending the oak tree
and stripping the forest bare.

The God of glory thunders.
In his temple they all cry: "Glory!"
The Lord sat enthroned over the flood;
the Lord sits as king for ever.

The Lord will give strength to his people,
the Lord will bless his people with peace.

Glory to the Father, and to the Son, and to the
    Holy Spirit:
as it was in the beginning, is now, and will be
    for ever. Amen.

Psalm-prayer

You live for ever, Lord and King. All things of
the earth justly sing your glory and honor.
Strengthen your people against evil that we may
rejoice in your peace and trust in your eternal
promise.

Reading

2 Thessalonians 3:10b-13

ANYONE who would not work should not eat.
We hear that some of you are unruly, not
keeping busy but acting like busy-bodies. We
enjoin all such, and we urge them strongly in the
Lord Jesus Christ, to earn the food they eat by
working quietly. You must never grow weary of
doing what is right, brothers.

Responsory

Blessed be the Lord our God,
blessed from age to age.
— Blessed be the Lord our God,
blessed from age to age.
His marvelous works are beyond compare,
— blessed from age to age.
Glory to the Father. . . .
— Blessed be the . . .

Canticle of Zechariah

Ant.   Blessed be the Lord our God.

(Turn to p. 130)

Intercessions

WE ESTEEM Christ above all men, for he was
filled with grace and the Holy Spirit. In
faith let us implore him:
  Give us your Spirit, Lord.
Grant us a peaceful day,
— when evening comes we will praise you with
joy and purity of heart.
Let your splendor rest upon us today,
— direct the work of our hands.
May your face shine upon us and keep us in peace,
— may your strong arm protect us.
Look kindly on all who put their trust in our
prayers,
— fill them with every bodily and spiritual grace.
Our Father . . .

Prayer

FATHER,
   may everything we do
begin with your inspiration
and continue with your saving help.
Let our work always find its origin in you
and through you reach completion.

We ask this through our Lord Jesus Christ, your
   Son,
who lives and reigns with you and the Holy
   Spirit,
one God, for ever and ever.

(Turn to p. 141)

MONDAY EVENING

Reflection

THE voices speaking to the soul in the opening verses of Psalm 11 are voices we hear too: "Fly like a bird to its mountain."

Often as we look back in the evening over the uneven picture of our day, fear and discouragement speak to us like this: Flee!

You have done nothing today, they say. Nothing but hurt and disappointment, and still so much to do. Your ideals are unattainable; your hopes are misplaced. Give up, they say. Escape!

"In the Lord I have taken my refuge" (Ps 11).

The Lord, our refuge, does not tell us to escape from life however. He is a warrior who marches with those engaged in life's struggles. To draw on his strength we must continue in the battle, not retreat.

Psalm 15 lists basic guiding principles for involving ourselves in life. Justice, truthfulness and constancy are not easy to practice. They are the virtues of a warrior, and we who follow Christ must live them "to be holy and blameless in his sight."

"By the might of his glory you will be endowed with the strength needed to stand fast, even to endure joyfully whatever may come . . ." (Colossians 1:11).

EVENING PRAYER

G OD, come to my assistance.
— Lord, make haste to help me.
Glory to the Father, and to the Son, and to the
Holy Spirit:
— as it was in the beginning, is now, and will
be for ever. Amen. Alleluia.

Hymn no. 26 or see Guide, 348.

The Lord looks ten-der - ly on those who are poor.

Psalm 11

God is the unfailing support of the just

*Blessed are those who hunger and thirst for jus-
tice; they shall be satisfied* (Matthew 5:6).

I N THE Lord I have taken my refuge.
How can you say to my soul:
"Fly like a bird to its mountain.

See the wicked bracing their bow;
they are fixing their arrows on the string
to shoot upright men in the dark.
Foundations once destroyed, what can the
just do?"

The Lord is in his holy temple,
the Lord, whose throne is in heaven.
His eyes look down on the world;
his gaze tests mortal men.

The Lord tests the just and the wicked:
the lover of violence he hates.
He sends fire and brimstone on the wicked;
he sends a scorching wind as their lot.

The Lord is just and loves justice:
the upright shall see his face.

Glory to the Father, and to the Son, and to the
Holy Spirit:
as it was in the beginning, is now, and will be
for ever. Amen.

Psalm-prayer
Lord God, you search the hearts of all, both
the good and the wicked. May those who are in
danger for love of you, find security in you now,
and, in the day of judgment, may they rejoice in
seeing you face to face.

Psalm 15

Who is worthy to stand in God's presence?

*You have come to Mount Zion, to the city of the
living God* (Hebrews 12:22).

LORD, who shall be admitted to your tent
and dwell on your holy mountain?

He who walks without fault;
he who acts with justice
and speaks the truth from his heart;
he who does not slander with his tongue;

he who does no wrong to his brother,
who casts no slur on his neighbor,
who holds the godless in disdain,
but honors those who fear the Lord;

he who keeps his pledge, come what may;
who takes no interest on a loan
accepts no bribes against the innocent.
Such a man will stand firm for ever.

Glory to the Father, and to the Son, and to the
   Holy Spirit:
as it was in the beginning, is now, and will be
   for ever. Amen.

Psalm-prayer

   Make our lives blameless, Lord. Help us to do
what is right and to speak what is true, that we
may dwell in your tent and find rest on your holy
mountain.

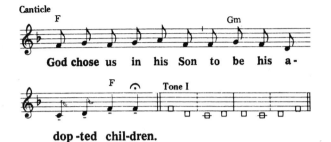

Canticle

God chose us   in   his   Son   to   be   his a -

dop -ted chil-dren.

Canticle: Ephesians 1:3-10

God our Savior

PRAISED be the God and Father
    of our Lord Jesus Christ,
who has bestowed on us in Christ
every spiritual blessing in the heavens.

God chose us in him
before the world began
to be holy
and blameless in his sight.

He predestined us
to be his adopted sons through Jesus Christ,
such was his will and pleasure,
that all might praise the glorious favor
he has bestowed on us in his beloved.

In him and through his blood, we have been
    redeemed,
and our sins forgiven,
so immeasurably generous
is God's favor to us.

God has given us the wisdom
to understand fully the mystery,
the plan he was pleased
to decree in Chirst.

A plan to be carried out
in Christ, in the fullness of time,
to bring all things into one in him,
in the heavens and on earth.

Glory to the Father, and to the Son, and to the
Holy Spirit:
as it was in the beginning, is now, and will be
for ever. Amen.

Reading

Colossians 1:9b-11

MAY you attain full knowledge of God's will through perfect wisdom and spiritual insight. Then you will lead a life worthy of the Lord and pleasing to him in every way. You will multiply good works of every sort and grow in the knowledge of God. By the might of his glory you will be endowed with the strength needed to stand fast, even to endure joyfully whatever may come.

Responsory

Lord, you alone can heal me, for I have grieved
you by my sins.
— Lord, you alone can heal me, for I have grieved
you by my sins.
Once more I say: O Lord, have mercy on me,
— for I have grieved you by my sins.
Glory to the Father . . .
— Lord, you alone . . .

Canticle of Mary

Ant.   My soul proclaims the greatness of the
Lord, for he has looked with favor on his
lowly servant.

(Turn to p. 131)

Intercessions

GOD has made an everlasting covenant with
his people, and he never ceases to bless them.
Grateful for these gifts, we confidently direct
our prayer to him:
Lord, bless your people.
Save your people, Lord,
—and bless your inheritance.
Gather into one body all who bear the name of
Christian,
—that the world may believe in Christ whom
you have sent.
Give our friends and our loved ones a share in
divine life,
—let them be symbols of Christ before men.
Show your love to those who are suffering,
—open their eyes to the vision of your revelation.
Be compassionate to those who have died,
—welcome them into the company of the faithful departed.

Our Father . . .

Prayer

FATHER,
may this evening pledge of our service to you
bring you glory and praise.

For our salvation you looked with favor
on the lowliness of the Virgin Mary;
lead us to the fullness of the salvation
you have prepared for us.

We ask this through our Lord Jesus Christ, your
    Son,
who lives and reigns with you and the Holy Spirit,
one God, for ever and ever.

(Dismissal, p. 141)

TUESDAY MORNING

Reflection

THE day is before us. God is within it already, waiting in creation and in the hours which will unfold before us according to the "plans of his heart" (Psalm 33:9). Yet, he also waits till we bring him to this day.

Psalm 24, a processional psalm, celebrates these two themes. It is the song of the ancient Israelites as they carried the Ark of the Covenant into the Temple bearing the Lord with them in procession. We, too, bear God himself where we go today, and consequently the ground itself on which we walk must become holy. God is present in the world we enter today, yet he seeks human hearts and minds and actions to manifest his presence in a unique way. We cannot do this simply through physical living, however. Our hearts and desires are the great instruments that reveal him.

When we hear the cries of the psalm, "O gates, lift high your heads. . . . Let him enter, the king of glory!" we need not think only of the gates of a special place. Perhaps we are asking that the gates of routine, of limited life, of sin be lifted; that what obstructs and diminishes our power to bring the Lord where we go may be removed, so that the "King of Glory" may be revealed.

The revelation of God in our lives becomes more difficult in the circumstances that the Song of Tobit describes: a land of exile. Like Tobit, we must praise God in that difficult land "and show his power and majesty to a sinful nation."

Psalm 33 returns to the opening theme of Psalm 24. The Lord is already present in his creation and in the movement of history. Even the place of exile is in his power.

MORNING PRAYER

LORD, open my lips.
— And my mouth will proclaim your praise.

Glory to, etc.:   — as it was, etc.

Ant.   Come, let us worship our mighty King and Lord.

Invitatory psalm, p 128.
Hymn no. 21 or see Guide, 348.

Antiphon

The man whose deeds are blame-less and whose heart

is   pure will climb the moun-tain of the Lord.

Tone I   Tone II

Psalm 24

The Lord's entry into his temple

Christ opened heaven for us in the manhood he assumed (Saint Irenaeus).

THE Lord's is the earth and its fullness,
the world and all its peoples.
It is he who set it on the seas;
on the waters he made it firm.

Who shall climb the mountain of the Lord?
Who shall stand in his holy place?
The man with clean hands and pure heart,
who desires not worthless things,
who has not sworn so as to deceive his neighbor.

He shall receive blessings from the Lord
and reward from the God who saves him.
Such are the men who seek him,
seek the face of the God of Jacob.

O gates, lift high your heads;
grow higher, ancient doors.
Let him enter, the king of glory!

Who is the king of glory?
The Lord, the mighty, the valiant,
the Lord, the valiant in war.

O gates, lift high your heads;
grow higher, ancient doors.
Let him enter, the king of glory!

Who is he, the king of glory?
He, the Lord of armies,
he is the king of glory.

Glory to the Father, and to the Son, and to the
  Holy Spirit:
as it was in the beginning, is now, and will be
  for ever. Amen.

Psalm-prayer

King of glory, Lord of power and might,
cleanse our hearts from all sin, preserve the innocence of our hands, and keep our minds from
vanity, so that we may deserve your blessing in
your holy place.

Praise the e - ter - nal King in all your deeds.

Canticle: Tobit 13:1-8

God afflicts but only to heal

*Blessed be the God and Father of our Lord Jesus
Christ, who in his great love for us has brought
us to a new birth* (1 Peter 1:3).

BLESSED be God who lives forever,
    because his kingdom lasts for all ages.

For he scourges and then has mercy;
he casts down to the depths of the nether
    world,
and he brings up from the great abyss.
No one can escape his hand.

Praise him, you Israelites, before the Gentiles,
for though he has scattered you among them,
he has shown you his greatness even there.

Exalt him before every living being,
because he is the Lord our God,
our Father and God forever,

He scourged you for your iniquities,
but will again have mercy on you all.
He will gather you from all the Gentiles
among whom you have been scattered.

When you turn back to him with all your
    heart,
to do what is right before him,
then he will turn back to you,
and no longer hide his face from you.

So now consider what he has done for you,
and praise him with full voice.
Bless the Lord of righteousness,
and exalt the King of the ages.

In the land of my exile I praise him,
and show his power and majesty to a sinful
    nation.
"Turn back, you sinners! do the right before
    him:
perhaps he may look with favor upon you
and show you mercy.

    "As for me, I exalt my God,
and my spirit rejoices in the King of heaven.
Let all men speak of his majesty,
and sing his praises in Jerusalem."

Glory to the Father, and to the Son, and to the
　Holy Spirit:
as it was in the beginning, is now, and will be
　for ever. Amen.

The loy-al heart must praise the Lord.

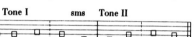

Psalm 33

Song of praise for God's continual care

Through the Word all things were made (John
1:3).

RING out your joy to the Lord, O you just;
for praise is fitting for loyal hearts.

Give thanks to the Lord upon the harp,
with a ten-stringed lute sing him songs.
O sing him a song that is new,
play loudly, with all your skill.

For the word of the Lord is faithful
and all his works to be trusted.
The Lord loves justice and right
and fills the earth with his love.

By his word the heavens were made,
by the breath of his mouth all the stars.
He collects the waves of the ocean;
he stores up the depths of the sea.

Let all the earth fear the Lord,
all who live in the world revere him.
He spoke; and it came to be.
He commanded; it sprang into being.

He frustrates the designs of the nations,
he defeats the plans of the peoples.
His own designs shall stand for ever,
the plans of his heart from age to age.

They are happy, whose God is the Lord,
the people he has chosen as his own.
From the heavens the Lord looks forth,
he sees all the children of men.

From the place where he dwells he gazes
on all the dwellers on the earth,
he who shapes the hearts of them all
and considers all their deeds.

A king is not saved by his army,
nor a warrior preserved by his strength.
A vain hope for safety is the horse;
despite its power it cannot save.

The Lord looks on those who revere him,
on those who hope in his love,
to rescue their souls from death,
to keep them alive in famine.

Our soul is waiting for the Lord.
The Lord is our help and our shield.
In him do our hearts find joy.
We trust in his holy name.

May your love be upon us, O Lord,
as we place all our hope in you.

Glory to the Father, and to the Son, and to the
Holy Spirit:
as it was in the beginning, is now, and will be
for ever. Amen.

Psalm-prayer

Nourish your people, Lord, for we hunger for
your word. Rescue us from the death of sin and
fill us with your mercy, that we may share your
presence and the joys of all the saints.

Reading

Romans 13:11b, 12-13a

IT IS now the hour for you to wake from sleep.
The night is far spent; the day draws near.
Let us cast off deeds of darkness and put on the
armor of light. Let us live honorably as in day-
light.

Responsory

My God stands by me, all my trust is in him.
— My God stands by me, all my trust is in him.
I find refuge in him, and I am truly free.
— all my trust is in him.
Glory to the Father . . .
— My God stands . . . .

Canticle of Zechariah

Ant.   God has raised up for us a mighty Savior,
as he promised through the words of his
holy prophets.

(Turn to p. 130)

Intercessions

BELOVED brothers and sisters, we share a heavenly calling under Christ, our high priest. Let us praise him with shouts of joy:
Lord, our God and our Savior.

Almighty King, through baptism you conferred on us a royal priesthood,
— inspire us to offer you a continual sacrifice of praise.

Help us to keep your commandments,
— that through the power of the Holy Spirit we may live in you and you in us.

Give us your eternal wisdom,
— to be with us today and to guide us.

May our companions today be free of sorrow,
— and filled with joy.

Our Father . . .

Prayer

GOD our Father,
hear our morning prayer
and let the radiance of your love
scatter the gloom of our hearts.
The light of heaven's love has restored us to life:
free us from the desires that belong to darkness.

We ask this through our Lord Jesus Christ, your Son,
who lives and reigns with you and the Holy Spirit,
one God, for ever and ever.

(Dismissal, p. 141)

TUESDAY EVENING
Reflection

TWO royal psalms begin this evening's prayer. Psalm 20 is an ancient Jewish prayer asking that the king be victorious in battle. Psalm 21 is a prayer of thanksgiving for a victory the king has achieved.

Both these psalms reveal the strong bond between the Israelites and their king. As God's anointed, the king lifted the spirits of his people and gave them hope. He was the rallying point of the nation, which shared his cause and achievements.

As Christians, we relate this way to Christ, whose life and destiny commingle with ours. The passion of Christ, his great battle, still goes on in us, the Body of Christ on earth. Similarly, we share in his resurrection and victory. In these two royal psalms, therefore, we pray in solidarity with Christ, our King.

The Canticle from Revelation, too, proclaims our present and future union in Jesus Christ. What that union will bring we have yet to see. God has promised that "we shall be like him . . . as he is" (1 John 3:2)—"a kingdom and priests to serve our God" (Revelation 5:10), sharing the power and glory of Christ.

Our lives are not small and insignificant. We are not isolated and alone. The psalms, readings *and prayers for this evening remind us of the dignity and destiny we share with Christ, our Lord.*

EVENING PRAYER

GOD, come to my assistance.
— Lord, make haste to help me.
Glory to the Father, and to the Son, and to the Holy Spirit:
— as it was in the beginning, is now, and will be for ever. Amen. Alleluia.

Hymn no. 13 or see Guide, 348.

God has crowned his Christ with vic - to - ry.

Psalm 20
A prayer for the king's victory

Whoever calls upon the name of the Lord will be saved (Acts 2:21).

MAY the Lord answer in time of trial;
may the name of Jacob's God protect you.

May he send you help from his shrine
and give you support from Zion.
May he remember all your offerings
and receive your sacrifice with favor.

May he give you your heart's desire
and fulfill every one of your plans.

May we ring out our joy at your victory
and rejoice in the name of our God.
May the Lord grant all your prayers.

I am sure now that the Lord
will give victory to his anointed,
will reply from his holy heaven
with the mighty victory of his hand.

Some trust in chariots or horses,
but we in the name of the Lord.
They will collapse and fall,
but we shall hold and stand firm.

Give victory to the king, O Lord,
give answer on the day we call.

Glory to the Father, and to the Son, and to the
  Holy Spirit:
as it was in the beginning, is now, and will be
  for ever. Amen.

Psalm-prayer

Lord, you accepted the perfect sacrifice of
your Son upon the cross. Hear us during times
of trouble and protect us by the power of his
name, that we who share his struggle on earth
may merit a share in his victory.

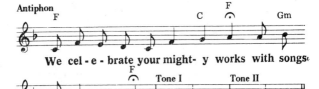

We cel - e - brate your might- y works with songs
of praise, O Lord.

Psalm 21:2-8, 14

Thanksgiving for the king's victory

He accepted life that he might rise and live for ever (Saint Hilary).

O LORD, your strength gives joy to the king;
how your saving help makes him glad!
You have granted him his heart's desire;
you have not refused the prayer of his lips.

You came to meet him with the blessings of success,
you have set on his head a crown of pure gold.
He asked you for life and this you have given,
days that will last from age to age.

Your saving help has given him glory.
You have laid upon him majesty and splendor,
you have granted your blessings to him for ever.
You have made him rejoice with the joy of your presence.

The king has put his trust in the Lord:
through the mercy of the Most High he shall stand firm.
O Lord, arise in your strength;
we shall sing and praise your power.

Glory to the Father, and to the Son, and to the Holy Spirit:
as it was in the beginning, is now, and will be for ever. Amen.

Psalm-prayer

Father, you have given us life on this earth and have met us with the grace of redemption. Bestow your greatest blessing on us, the fullness of eternal life.

Antiphon

Lord, you have made us　a King-dom and priests

for God our　Fa - ther.

Canticle: Revelation 4:11; 5:9, 10, 12

Redemption hymn

O LORD our God, you are worthy
　to receive glory and honor and power.

For you have created all things;
　by your will they came to be and were made.

Worthy are you, O Lord,
　to receive the scroll and break open its seals.

For you were slain;
　with your blood you purchased for God
　men of every race and tongue,
　of every people and nation.

You made of them a kingdom,
　and priests to serve our God,
　and they shall reign on the earth.

Worthy is the Lamb that was slain
to receive power and riches,
wisdom and strength,
honor and glory and praise.

Glory to the Father, and to the Son, and to the
Holy Spirit:
as it was in the beginning, is now, and will be
for ever. Amen.

Reading

1 John 3:1a, 2

SEE what love the Father has bestowed on us
in letting us be called children of God!
Yet that is what we are.
Dearly beloved,
we are God's children now;
what we shall later be has not yet come to light.
We know that when it comes to light
we shall be like him
for we shall see him as he is.

Responsory

Through all eternity, O Lord, your promise
stands unshaken.
—Through all eternity, O Lord, your promise
stands unshaken.

Your faithfulness will never fail;
—your promise stands unshaken.

Glory to the Father . . .
—Through all eternity . . .

Canticle of Mary

Ant.   My spirit rejoices in God my Savior.

(Turn to p. 131)

Intercessions

LET us praise Christ the Lord, who lives among us, the people he redeemed, and let us say:

Lord, hear our prayer.

Lord, king and ruler of nations, be with all your people and their governments,

— inspire them to pursue the good of all according to your law.

You made captive our captivity,

— to our brothers who are enduring bodily or spiritual chains, grant the freedom of the sons of God.

May our young people be concerned with remaining blameless in your sight,

— and may they generously follow your call.

May our children imitate your example,

— and grow in wisdom and grace.

Accept our dead brothers and sisters into your eternal kingdom,

— where we hope to reign with you.

Our Father . . .

Prayer

ALMIGHTY God,
we give you thanks
for bringing us safely
to this evening hour.
May this lifting up of our hands in prayer
be a sacrifice pleasing in your sight.

We ask this through our Lord Jesus Christ, your Son

who lives . . . for ever and ever.

(Dismissal, p. 141)

WEDNESDAY MORNING

Reflection

PSALM 36 begins this morning's prayer cautioning us to beware of sin.

"Sin speaks to the sinner in the depths of his heart."

Sin and evil cast their dark spell everywhere, but their favorite home is the human heart. There they foster self-deception, hostility toward others and forgetfulness of God. The sinner within us knows how enticing the call of wickedness is.

God's goodness, however, is stronger no matter how powerful sin may appear. The light of his grace brightens the heights and the depths, overcoming all darkness.

The story of Judith, the Jewess who killed the powerful oppressive king, Holofernes, reveals the way God's mercy overturns evil. Using the frailest and weakest of his people—but one who depended on him—God destroyed a stronghold of sin. The song of Judith in this morning's prayer is the song of one who triumphed over invincible odds because she hoped in the Lord.

We should be aware of sin as we go on our way today. But, more importantly, we should rejoice in God's strong grace, which is given to us.

Psalm 47, the final psalm, further celebrates God's mighty power present in Jesus Christ, the King of all nations.

MORNING PRAYER

L ORD, open my lips.
— And my mouth will proclaim your praise.

Glory to, etc.:   — as it was, etc.

Ant.   Come, let us worship before the Lord, our maker.

Invitatory psalm, p. 128.
Hymn no. 25 or see Guide, 348.

Canticle

O Lord, in your light we see light it - self.

Psalm 36

The malice of sinners and God's goodness

No follower of mine wanders in the dark; he shall have the light of life (John 8:12).

S IN speaks to the sinner
in the depths of his heart.
There is no fear of God
before his eyes.

He so flatters himself in his mind
that he knows not his guilt.

In his mouth are mischief and deceit.
All wisdom is gone.

He so flatters himself in his mind
as he lies on his bed.
He has set his foot on evil ways,
he clings to what is evil.

Your love, Lord, reaches to heaven;
your truth to the skies.
Your justice is like God's mountain,
your judgments like the deep.

To both man and beast you give protection.
O Lord, how precious is your love.
My God, the sons of men
find refuge in the shelter of your wings.

They feast on the riches of your house;
they drink from the stream of your delight.
In you is the source of life
and in your light we see light.

Keep on loving those who know you,
doing justice for upright hearts.
Let the foot of the proud not crush me
nor the hand of the wicked cast me out.

See how the evil-doers fall!
Flung down, they shall never rise.

Glory to the Father, and to the Son, and to the
  Holy Spirit:
as it was in the beginning, is now, and will be
  for ever. Amen.

Psalm-prayer

Lord, you are the source of unfailing light. Give us true knowledge of your mercy so that we may renounce our pride and be filled with the riches of your house.

Canticle

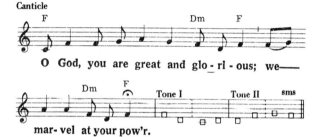

O God, you are great and glo - ri - ous; we——

mar- vel at your pow'r.

Canticle: Judith 16:2-3a, 13-15

God who created the world takes care of his people

They were singing a new song (Revelation 5:9)

STRIKE up the instruments,
a song to my God with timbrels,
chant to the Lord with cymbals.
Sing to him a new song,
exalt and acclaim his name.

A new hymn I will sing to my God.
O Lord, great are you and glorious,
wonderful in power and unsurpassable.

Let your every creature serve you;
for you spoke, and they were made,
you sent forth your spirit, and they were
  created;
no one can resist your word.

The mountains to their bases, and the seas,
    are shaken;
the rocks, like wax, melt before your glance.
But to those who fear you,
    you are merciful.

Glory to the Father, and to the Son, and to the
    Holy Spirit:
as it was in the beginning, is now, and will be
    for ever. Amen.

Antiphon

Ex - ult   in God's pre-sence with hymns of praise

Tone I   Tone II   8ms

Psalm 47

The Lord Jesus is King of all

*He is seated at the right hand of the Father, and
his kingdom will have no end.*

ALL peoples, clap your hands,
    cry to God with shouts of joy!
For the Lord, the Most High, we must fear,
great king over all the earth.

He subdues peoples under us
and nations under our feet.
Our inheritance, our glory, is from him,
given to Jacob out of love.

God goes up with shouts of joy;
the Lord goes up with trumpet blast.

Sing praise for God, sing praise,
sing praise to our king, sing praise.

God is king of all the earth.
Sing praise with all your skill.
God is king over the nations;
God reigns on his holy throne.

The princes of the peoples are assembled
with the people of Abraham's God.
The rulers of the earth belong to God,
to God who reigns over all.

Glory to the Father, and to the Son, and to the
   Holy Spirit:
as it was in the beginning, is now, and will be
   for ever. Amen.

Psalm-prayer

God, King of all peoples and all ages, it is your
victory we celebrate as we sing with all the skill
at our command. Help us always to overcome
evil by good, that we may rejoice in your triumph
for ever.

Reading

Tobit 4:15a, 16a, 18a, 19

DO TO no one what you yourself dislike. Give
   to the hungry some of your bread, and to the
naked some of your clothing. Seek counsel from
every wise man. At all times bless the Lord God,
and ask him to make all your paths straight and
to grant success to all your endeavors and plans.

Responsory

Incline my heart according to your will, O God.
—Incline my heart according to your will, O
   God.
Speed my steps along your path,
—according to your will, O God.
Glory to the Father . . .
—Incline my heart . . .

Canticle of Zechariah

Ant.   Show us your mercy, Lord; remember
       your holy covenant.

(Turn to p. 130)

Intercessions

LET us give thanks to Christ and offer him
   continued praise, for he sanctifies us and
   calls us his brothers:
   Lord, help your brothers to grow in holiness.
With single-minded devotion we dedicate the
   beginnings of this day to the honor of your
   resurrection,
—may we make the whole day pleasing to you
   by our works of holiness.
As a sign of your love, you renew each day for
   the sake of our well-being and happiness,
—renew us daily for the sake of your glory.
Teach us today to recognize your presence in all
   men,
—especially in the poor and in those who
   mourn.
Grant that we may live today in peace with all
   men,

— never rendering evil for evil.

Our Father . . .

Prayer

GOD our Savior,
hear our morning prayer:
help us to follow the light
and live the truth.
In you we have been born again
as sons and daughters of light:
may we be your witnesses before all the world.

We ask this through our Lord Jesus Christ, your
   Son,
who lives and reigns with you and the Holy
   Spirit,
one God, for ever and ever.

(Dismissal, p. 141)

WEDNESDAY EVENING

Reflection

NO ONE ends a day without some scars. Count them within yourself. The day inflicts its wounds, sometimes painful indeed. Any account of twenty-four hours must list our experiences of hostility and misunderstanding from the world around us, as well as of conflict within.

Then, too, what has been accomplished? Time has passed. Yet have we done anything significant? Perhaps the psalmist in Psalm 27 is speaking to God from sentiments like these, seeking comfort and steadying from him in the wearying experience of life.

The psalmist enters the temple to be refreshed by the loveliness of the Lord, to feel the security of resting in God, the Rock. Our place of refreshment is Christ, the living temple. "Come to me, all you who are weary and find life burdensome and I will refresh you" (Matthew 11:28).

The saints in their trials found shelter in the Passion of Christ. "Where can our frailty find rest and security if not in the wounds of Christ?" St. Bernard asks. In Christ, who suffered and died, God has become a compassionate companion to suffering humanity.

Psalm 27 ends with God's own strong words: "Hope in him, hold firm and take heart. Hope in the Lord!" The great canticle from Colossians affirms the basis for our hope: God has called us to his kingdom through Christ who redeemed

EVENING PRAYER

G OD, come to my assistance.
— Lord, make haste to help me.
Glory to the Father, and to the Son, and to the
   Holy Spirit:
— as it was in the beginning, is now, and will be
   for ever. Amen. Alleluia.

Hymn no. 18 or see Guide, 348.

The Lord is my light and my help; whom shall I fear?

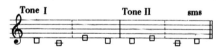

Psalm 27

God stands by us in dangers

God now truly dwells with men (Revelation 21:3)

I

T HE Lord is my light and my help;
   whom shall I fear?
The Lord is the stronghold of my life;
before whom shall I shrink?

When evil-doers draw near
to devour my flesh,
it is they, my enemies and foes,
who stumble and fall.

Though an army encamp against me
my heart would not fear.
Though war break out against me
even then would I trust.

There is one thing I ask of the Lord,
for this I long,
to live in the house of the Lord,
all the days of my life,
to savor the sweetness of the Lord,
to behold his temple.

For there he keeps me safe in his tent
in the day of evil.
He hides me in the shelter of his tent,
on a rock he sets me safe.

And now my head shall be raised
above my foes who surround me
and I shall offer within his tent
a sacrifice of joy.

I will sing and make music for the Lord.

Glory to the Father, and to the Son, and to the
  Holy Spirit:
as it was in the beginning, is now, and will be
  for ever. Amen.

I long to look on you, O' Lord; do not

turn your face from me.

II

O Lord, hear my voice when I call;
have mercy and answer.
Of you my heart has spoken:
"Seek his face."

It is your face, O Lord, that I seek;
hide not your face.
Dismiss not your servant in anger;
you have been my help.

Do not abandon or forsake me,
O God my help!
Though father and mother forsake me,
the Lord will receive me.

Instruct me, Lord, in your way;
on an even path lead me.
When they lie in ambush protect me
from my enemy's greed.
False witnesses rise against me,
breathing out fury.

I am sure I shall see the Lord's goodness
in the land of the living.
Hope in him, hold firm and take heart.
Hope in the Lord!

Glory to the Father, and to the Son, and to the
Holy Spirit:
as it was in the beginning, is now, and will be
for ever. Amen.

Psalm-prayer

Father, you protect and strengthen those who hope in you; you heard the cry of your Son and kept him safe in your tent in the day of evil. Grant that your servants who seek your face in times of trouble may see your goodness in the land of the living.

Canticle

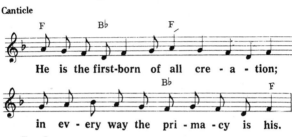

He is the first-born of all cre - a - tion;
in ev - ery way the pri - ma - cy is his.

Tone I

Canticle: Colossians 1:11-20

Christ the first-born of all creation and the first-born from the dead

LET us give thanks to the Father
for having made you worthy
to share the lot of the saints
in light.

He rescued us
from the power of darkness
and brought us
into the kingdom of his beloved Son.
Through him we have redemption,
the forgiveness of our sins.

He is the image of the invisible God,
the first-born of all creatures.
In him everything in heaven and on earth
    was created,
things visible and invisible.

All were created through him;
all were created for him.
He is before all else that is.
In him everything continues in being.

It is he who is head of the body, the church!
he who is the beginning,
the first-born of the dead,
so that primacy may be his in everything.

It pleased God to make absolute fulness re-
    side in him
and, by means of him, to reconcile everything
    in his person,
both on earth and in the heavens,
making peace through the blood of his
    cross.

Glory to the Father, and to the Son, and to the
    Holy Spirit:
as it was in the beginning, is now, and will be
    for ever. Amen.

Reading

James 1:22, 25

ACT on this word. If all you do is listen to it,
you are deceiving yourselves. There is, on
the other hand, the man who peers into freedom's ideal law and abides by it. He is no forget-

ful listener, but one who carries out the law in practice. Blest will this man be in whatever he does.

Responsory

Claim me once more as your own, Lord, and have mercy on me.
— Claim me once more as your own, Lord, and have mercy on me.
Do not abandon me with the wicked;
— have mercy on me.
Glory to the Father . . .
— Claim me once . . .

Canticle of Mary

Ant.   The Almighty has done great things for me, and holy is his Name.

(Turn to p. 131)

Intercessions

IN ALL we do, let the name of the Lord be praised, for he surrounds his chosen people with boundless love. Let our prayer rise up to him:
Lord, show us your love.
Remember your Church, Lord,
— keep her from every evil and let her grow to the fullness of your love.
Let the nations recognize you as the one true God,
— and Jesus your Son, as the Messiah whom you sent.
Grant prosperity to our neighbors,
— give them life and happiness for ever.

Console those who are burdened with oppressive work and daily hardships,
— preserve the dignity of workers.
Open wide the doors of your compassion to those
   who have died today,
— and in your mercy receive them into your
   kingdom.
Our Father . . .

Prayer

L ORD,
   watch over us by day and by night.
In the midst of life's countless changes
strengthen us with your never-changing love.

We ask this through our Lord Jesus Christ, your
   Son,
who lives and reigns with you and the Holy
   Spirit,
one God, for ever and ever.

(Dismissal, p. 141)

THURSDAY MORNING

Reflection

SAINT *Augustine calls Psalm 57, the first psalm for this morning's prayer, a prayer of Jesus Christ in his passion. It is our prayer, too, as members of Christ. "The whole Christ is speaking here; here is your voice too."*

Whatever conflict and suffering this day brings, we are prepared to meet it in Christ. "My heart is ready, O God."

The Canticle from Jeremiah is a song from exile. The weak, the poor in spirit, the sinner, gathered together by God's redeeming love, will make the journey to his kingdom. Poor as we are, we can rely on God's promise of strength for this day's journey.

The final psalm, 48, celebrates God's saving presence in Zion, his holy city. This is a favorite theme in the psalms.

God is indeed everywhere, but he is especially present in his people and his church.

Praise and appreciate God's gifts in those around you, this psalm proclaims. Recognize God's presence in those who are nearest you. Don't miss his power in what is closest to you.

Walk through Zion, walk all round it;
count the number of its towers.
Review all its ramparts,
examine its castles.

MORNING PRAYER

L ORD, open my lips.
 — And my mouth will proclaim your praise.

Glory to, etc.:   — as it was, etc.

Ant.   Come, let us worship the Lord, for he is
        our God.

Invitatory psalm, p 128.
Hymn no. 19 or see Guide, 348.

Antiphon

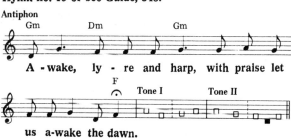

A - wake, ly - re and harp, with praise let

us a-wake the dawn.

Psalm 57

Morning prayer in affliction

This psalm tells of our Lord's passion (Saint
Augustine).

H AVE mercy on me, God, have mercy
  for in you my soul has taken refuge.
In the shadow of your wings I take refuge
till the storms of destruction pass by.

I call to God the Most High,
to God who has always been my help.
May he send from heaven and save me
and shame those who assail me.

May God send his truth and his love.
My soul lies down among lions,
who would devour the sons of men.
Their teeth are spears and arrows,
their tongue a sharpened sword.

O God, arise above the heavens;
may your glory shine on earth!

They laid a snare for my steps,
my soul was bowed down.
They dug a pit in my path
but fell in it themselves.

My heart is ready, O God,
my heart is ready.
I will sing, I will sing your praise.
Awake, my soul,
awake, lyre and harp,
I will awake the dawn.

I will thank you, Lord, among the peoples,
among the nations I will praise you
for your love reaches to the heavens
and your truth to the skies.

O God, arise above the heavens;
may your glory shine on earth!

Glory to the Father, and to the Son, and to the
Holy Spirit:
as it was in the beginning, is now, and will be
for ever. Amen.

Psalm-prayer

Lord, send your mercy and your truth to
rescue us from the snares of the devil, and we
will praise you among the peoples and proclaim

you to the nations, happy to be known as companions of your Son.

Canticle

My peo-ple, says the Lord, will be filled—

with my bless-ings.

Canticle: Jeremiah 31:10-14

The happiness of a people who have been redeemed

Jesus was to die . . . to gather God's scattered children into one fold (John 11:51, 52).

HEAR the word of the Lord, O nations,
proclaim it on distant coasts, and say:
He who scattered Israel, now gathers them
together,
he guards them as a shepherd his flock.

The Lord shall ransom Jacob,
he shall redeem him from the hand of his
conqueror.

Shouting, they shall mount the heights of
Zion,
they shall come streaming to the Lord's
blessings:
the grain, the vine, and the oil,
the sheep and the oxen;

they themselves shall be like watered gardens,
never again shall they languish.

Then the virgins shall make merry and dance,
and young men and old as well.
I will turn their mourning into joy,
I will console and gladden them after their sorrows.
I will lavish choice portions upon the priests,
and my people shall be filled with my blessings,
says the Lord.

Glory to the Father, and to the Son, and to the Holy Spirit:
as it was in the beginning, is now, and will be for ever. Amen.

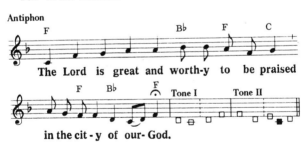

Antiphon

The Lord is great and worth-y to be praised in the cit - y of our- God.

Psalm 48

Thanksgiving for the people's deliverance

He took me up a high mountain and showed me Jerusalem, God's holy city (Revelation 21:10).

THE Lord is great and worthy to be praised in the city of our God.

His holy mountain rises in beauty,
the joy of all the earth.

Mount Zion, true pole of the earth,
the Great King's city!
God, in the midst of its citadels,
has shown himself its stronghold.

For the kings assembled together,
together they advanced.
They saw; at once they were astounded;
dismayed, they fled in fear.

A trembling seized them there,
like the pangs of birth.
By the east wind you have destroyed
the ships of Tarshish.

As we have heard, so we have seen
in the city of our God,
in the city of the Lord of hosts
which God upholds for ever.

O God, we ponder your love
within your temple.
Your praise, O God, like your name
reaches to the ends of the earth.

With justice your right hand is filled.
Mount Zion rejoices;
the people of Judah rejoice
at the sight of your judgments.

Walk through Zion, walk all round it;
count the number of its towers.
Review all its ramparts,
examine its castles,

that you may tell the next generation
that such is our God,
our God for ever and always.
It is he who leads us

Glory to the Father, and to the Son, and to the
Holy Spirit:
as it was in the beginning, is now, and will be
for ever. Amen.

Psalm-prayer

Father, the body of your risen Son is the temple not made by human hands and the defending wall of the new Jerusalem. May this holy city, built of living stones, shine with spiritual radiance and witness to your greatness in the sight of all nations.

Reading

Isaiah 66:1-2

THUS says the Lord:
The heavens are my throne,
and the earth is my footstool.
What kind of house can you build for me;
what is to be my resting place?
My hand made all these things
when all of them came to be, says the Lord.
This is the one whom I approve:
the lowly and afflicted man who trembles at
my word.

Responsory

From the depths of my heart I cry to you: hear
me, O Lord.
—From the depths of my heart I cry to you;

hear me, O Lord.
I will do what you desire;
—hear me, O Lord.
Glory to the Father . . .
—From the depths . . .

Canticle of Zechariah

Ant.   Let us serve the Lord in holiness, and he
will save us from our enemies.

(Turn to p. 130)

Intercessions

THE Lord Jesus Christ has given us the light
of another day. In return we thank him as
we cry out:
Lord, bless us and bring us close to you.
You offered yourself in sacrifice for our sins,
—accept our intentions and our work today.
You bring us joy by the light of another day,
—let the morning star rise in our hearts.
Give us strength to be patient with those we
meet today,
—and so imitate you.
Make us aware of your mercy this morning,
Lord,
—and let your strength be our delight.

Our Father . . .   ### Prayer

ALL-POWERFUL and ever-living God,
at morning, noon, and evening we pray:
cast out from our hearts the darkness of sin
and bring us to the light of your truth,
Jesus Christ, who lives and reigns with you and
the Holy Spirit,
one God, for ever and ever. (Dismissal, p. 141)

THURSDAY EVENING

Reflection

WE CELEBRATE evening prayer, says St. Basil, to "give thanks for what has been given us, or what we have done well during the day." Blessings too numerous to mention call for our acknowledgment.

One of God's greatest blessings is the hope of eternal life we have in Jesus Christ, who promised that those who believe in him "even if they die, shall live."

Night's coming warns us of the coming of her sister, Death. The end of all our mortal days is foreshadowed in the end of this one.

With Christ we look for life beyond the grave, however, where mourning will be changed into dancing and sorrow into joy. (Psalm 30)

Even sin, the death of the soul, can be forgiven and new life imparted by God, if we but seek his forgiveness.

I will confess
my offense to the Lord.
And you, Lord, have forgiven
the guilt of my sin. (Psalm 32)

EVENING PRAYER

G OD, come to my assistance.
    — Lord, make haste to help me.
Glory to the Father, and to the Son, and to the
    Holy Spirit:
— as it was in the beginning, is now, and will be
    for ever. Amen. Alleluia.

Hymn no 20 or see Guide, 348.

I cried to you, Lord, and you healed me; I will

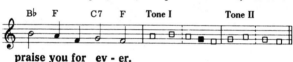

praise you for ev - er.

Psalm 30

Thanksgiving for deliverance from death

*Christ, risen in glory, gives continual thanks to
his Father* (Cassian).

I WILL praise you, Lord, you have rescued
    me
and have not let my enemies rejoice over me.

O Lord, I cried to you for help
and you, my God, have healed me.
O Lord, you have raised my soul from the
    dead,
restored me to life from those who sink into
    the grave.

Sing psalms to the Lord, you who love him,
give thanks to his holy name.
His anger lasts a moment; his favor through
    life.
At night there are tears, but joy comes with
    dawn.

I said to myself in my good fortune:
"Nothing will ever disturb me."
Your favor had set me on a mountain fast-
    ness,
then you hid your face and I was put to con-
    fusion.

To you, Lord, I cried,
to my God I made appeal:
"What profit would my death be, my going
    to the grave?
Can dust give you praise or proclaim your
    truth?"

The Lord listened and had pity.
The Lord came to my help.
For me you have changed my mourning into
    dancing,
you removed my sackcloth and clothed me
    with joy.
So my soul sings psalms to you unceasingly.
O Lord my God, I will thank you for ever.

Glory to the Father, and to the Son, and to the
    Holy Spirit:
as it was in the beginning, is now, and will be
    for ever. Amen.

Psalm-prayer

God our Father, glorious in giving life, and
even more glorious in restoring it, when his last
night on earth came, your Son shed tears of
blood, but dawn brought incomparable gladness.
Do not turn away from us, or we shall fall back
into dust, but rather turn our mourning into joy
by raising us up with Christ.

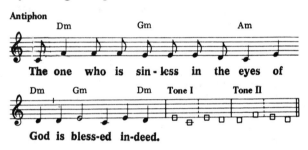

Antiphon

The one who is sin-less in the eyes of

God is bless-ed in-deed.

Psalm 32
They are happy whose sins are forgiven

*David speaks of the happiness of the man who
is holy in God's eyes not because of his own
worth, but because God has justified him*
(Romans 4:6).

HAPPY the man whose offense is forgiven,
whose sin is remitted.
O happy the man to whom the Lord
imputes no guilt,
in whose spirit is no guile.

I kept it secret and my frame was wasted.
I groaned all the day long
for night and day your hand

was heavy upon me.
Indeed, my strength was dried up
as by the summer's heat.

But now I have acknowledged my sins;
my guilt I did not hide.
I said: "I will confess
my offense to the Lord."
And you, Lord, have forgiven
the guilt of my sin.

So let every good man pray to you
in the time of need.
The floods of water may reach high
but him they shall not reach.
You are my hiding place, O Lord;
you save me from distress.
You surround me with cries of deliverance.

I will instruct you and teach you
the way you should go;
I will give you counsel
with my eye upon you.

Be not like horse and mule, unintelligent,
needing bridle and bit,
else they will not approach you.
Many sorrows has the wicked
but he who trusts in the Lord,
loving mercy surrounds him.

Rejoice, rejoice in the Lord,
exult, you just!
O come, ring out your joy,
all you upright of heart.

Glory to the Father, and to the Son, and to the
  Holy Spirit:

as it was in the beginning, is now, and will be
for ever. Amen.

Psalm-prayer

You desired, Lord, to keep from us your in-
dignation and so did not spare Jesus Christ, who
was wounded for our sins. We are your prodigal
children, but confessing our sins we come back
to you. Embrace us that we may rejoice in your
mercy together with Christ your beloved Son.

Canticle

The Fa-ther has giv - en— Christ all pow-er,
hon-or and King-ship; all peo-ple will o - bey him.

Tone I   Tone II

Canticle: Revelation 11:17-18; 12:10b-12a

The judgment of God

WE PRAISE you, the Lord God Almighty,
who is and who was.
You have assumed your great power,
you have begun your reign.

The nations have raged in anger,
but then came your day of wrath
and the moment to judge the dead:

the time to reward your servants the proph-
    ets
and the holy ones who revere you,
the great and the small alike.

Now have salvation and power come,
the reign of our God and the authority
of his Anointed One.
For the accuser of our brothers is cast out,
who night and day accused them before God.

They defeated him by the blood of the Lamb
and by the word of their testimony;
love for life did not deter them from death.
So rejoice, you heavens,
    and you that dwell therein!

Glory to the Father, and to the Son, and to the
    Holy Spirit:
as it was in the beginning, is now, and will be
    for ever. Amen.

Reading

1 Peter 1:6-9

THERE is cause for rejoicing here. You may
for a time have to suffer the distress of
many trials; but this is so that your faith, which
is more precious than the passing splendor of
fire-tried gold, may by its genuineness lead to
praise, glory, and honor when Jesus Christ appears. Although you have never seen him, you
love him, and without seeing you now believe in
him, and rejoice with inexpressible joy touched
with glory because you are achieving faith's
goal, your salvation.

Responsory

The Lord has given us food, bread of the finest
  wheat.
—The Lord has given us food, bread of the
  finest wheat.
Honey from the rock to our heart's content,
—bread of the finest wheat.

Glory to he Father . . .
—The Lord has . . .

Canticle of Mary

Ant.   God has cast down the mighty from their
        thrones, and has lifted up the lowly.

(Turn to p. 131)

Intercessions

OUR hope is in God, who gives us help. Let us
  call upon him, and say:
   Look kindly on your children, Lord.
Lord, our God, you made an eternal covenant
  with your people,
—keep us ever mindful of your mighty deeds.
Let your ordained ministers grow toward perfect
  love,
—and preserve your faithful people in unity by
  the bond of peace.
Be with us in our work of building the earthly
  city,
—that in building we may not labor in vain.
Send workers into your vineyard,
—and glorify your name among the nations.
Welcome into the company of your saints our
  relatives and benefactors who have died,
—may we share their happiness one day.
Our Father . . .

Prayer

FATHER,
   you illumine the night
and bring the dawn to scatter darkness.
Let us pass this night in safety,
free from Satan's power,
and rise when morning comes
to give you thanks and praise.

We ask this through our Lord Jesus Christ, your
   Son,
who lives and reigns with you and the Holy
   Spirit,
one God, for ever and ever.

(Dismissal, p. 141)

FRIDAY MORNING

Reflection

ANYONE searching his own heart knows the deposits of darkness and sin lying there, despite God's gifts and grace. To recognize ourselves as sinners is simply to recognize that which is weakest in ourselves. No, we do not always act for the best motives, nor do we always think the best thoughts. Jealousy, resentment, selfishness surface too often for us to deny they are part of us.

Ultimately, only God can cleanse us of our sins. His mercy we seek in Psalm 51.

I must pray for my own sinfulness, but there is a sinfulness in the society where I live, in its institutions, its customs, its ways of acting, causing us to be alienated from our God. The Prophet Isaiah calls us to turn from our idols and our foolishness and seek our God who waits to reveal himself to us.

Every prayer for mercy is made with the certainty of being heard. "Make me hear rejoicing and gladness, that the bones you have crushed may revive." The final psalm, Psalm 100, expresses our rejoicing and gladness. We can approach God confidently, through his Son, Jesus Christ. "We are his people, the sheep of his flock."

MORNING PRAYER

LORD, open my lips.
— And my mouth will proclaim your praise.

Glory to, etc.:   — as it was, etc.

Ant.   Come, let us give thanks to the Lord, for
his great love is without end.

Invitatory psalm, p. 128.

Hymn no. 17 or see Guide, 348.

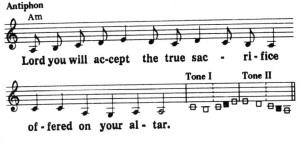

Antiphon

Lord you will ac-cept the true sac - ri-fice
of-fered on your al - tar.

Psalm 51

O God, have mercy on me

*Your inmost being must be renewed, and you
must put on the new man (Ephesians 4:23-24).*

HAVE mercy on me, God, in your kindness.
In your compassion blot out my offense.
O wash me more and more from my guilt
and cleanse me from my sin.

My offenses truly I know them;
my sin is always before me.
Against you, you alone, have I sinned;
what is evil in your sight I have done.

That you may be justified when you give sen-
    tence
and be without reproach when you judge.
O see, in guilt I was born,
a sinner was I conceived.

Indeed you love truth in the heart;
then in the secret of my heart teach me wis-
    dom.
O purify me, then I shall be clean;
O wash me, I shall be whiter than snow.

Make me hear rejoicing and gladness,
that the bones you have crushed may revive.
From my sins turn away your face
and blot out all my guilt.

A pure heart create for me, O God,
put a steadfast spirit within me.
Do not cast me away from your presence,
nor deprive me of your holy spirit.

Give me again the joy of your help;
with a spirit of fervor sustain me,
that I may teach transgressors your ways
and sinners may return to you.

O rescue me, God, my helper.
and my tongue shall ring out your goodness.
O Lord, open my lips
and my mouth shall declare your praise.

For in sacrifice you take no delight,
burnt offering from me you would refuse,
my sacrifice, a contrite spirit.
A humbled, contrite heart you will not spurn.

In your goodness, show favor to Zion:
rebuild the walls of Jerusalem.
Then you will be pleased with lawful sacrifice,
holocausts offered on your altar.

Glory to the Father, and to the Son, and to the
Holy Spirit:
as it was in the beginning, is now, and will be
for ever. Amen.

Psalm-prayer

Father, he who knew no sin was made sin for
us, to save us and restore us to your friendship.
Look upon our contrite heart and afflicted spirit
and heal our troubled conscience, so that in the
joy and strength of the Holy Spirit we may proclaim your praise and glory before all the nations.

Canticle

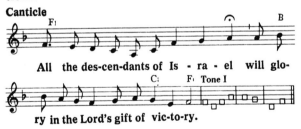

All the des-cen-dants of Is - ra - el will glory in the Lord's gift of vic-to-ry.

Canticle: Isaiah 45:15-25

People of all nations will become disciples of the Lord

Every knee shall bend at the name of Jesus
(Philippians 2:10).

TRULY with you God is hidden,
the God of Israel, the savior!
Those are put to shame and disgrace
who vent their anger against him.
Those go in disgrace
who carve images.

Israel, you are saved by the Lord, saved forever!
You shall never be put to shame or disgrace
in future ages.

For thus says the Lord,
the creator of the heavens,
who is God,
the designer and maker of the earth
who established it,
not creating it to be a waste,
but designing it to be lived in:

I am the Lord, and there is no other.
I have not spoken from hiding
nor from some dark place of the earth.
And I have not said to the descendants of
Jacob,
"Look for me in an empty waste."
I, the Lord, promise justice,
I foretell what is right.

Come and assemble, gather together,
you fugitives from among the Gentiles!
They are without knowledge who bear
wooden idols
and pray to gods that cannot save.

Come here and declare
in counsel together:
Who announced this from the beginning
and foretold it from of old?
Was it not I, the Lord,
besides whom there is no other God?
There is no just and saving God but me.

Turn to me and be safe,
all you ends of the earth,
for I am God; there is no other!

By myself I swear,
uttering my just decree
and my unalterable word:

To me every knee shall bend;
by me every tongue shall swear,
saying, "Only in the Lord
are just deeds and power.

Before him in shame shall come
all who vent their anger against him.
In the Lord shall be the vindication and the
     glory
of all the descendants of Israel."

Glory to the Father, and to the Son, and to the
    Holy Spirit:
as it was in the beginning, is now, and will be
    for ever. Amen.

Antiphon

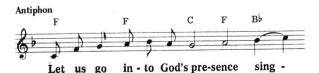

Let us go in-to God's pre-sence sing -

ing for joy.

Psalm 100

The joyful song of those entering God's temple

The Lord calls his ransomed people to sing songs of victory (Saint Athanasius).

CRY out with joy to the Lord, all the earth.
Serve the Lord with gladness.
Come before him, singing for joy.

Know that he, the Lord, is God.
He made us, we belong to him,
we are his people, the sheep of his flock.

Go within his gates, giving thanks.
Enter his courts with songs of praise.
Give thanks to him and bless his name.

Indeed, how good is the Lord,
eternal his merciful love.
He is faithful from age to age.

Glory to the Father, and to the Son, and to the
Holy Spirit:
as it was in the beginning, is now, and will be
for ever. Amen.

Psalm-prayer

With joy and gladness we cry out to you, Lord,
and ask you: open our hearts to sing your praises
and announce your goodness and truth.

Reading:

Ephesians 4:29-32

NEVER let evil talk pass your lips; say only the good things men need to hear, things that will really help them. Do nothing that will sadden the Holy Spirit with whom you were sealed against the day of redemption. Get rid of all bitterness, all passion and anger, harsh words, slander, and malice of every kind. In place of these, be kind to one another, compassionate, and mutually forgiving, just as God has forgiven you in Christ.

Responsory

At daybreak, be merciful to me.
— At daybreak, be merciful to me.
Make known to me the path that I must walk.
— Be merciful to me.
Glory to the Father . . .
— At daybreak, be . . .

Canticle of Zechariah

Ant. The Lord has come to his people and set them free.

(Turn to p. 130)

Intercessions

THROUGH his cross the Lord Jesus brought salvation to the human race. We adore him and in faith we call out to him:
Lord, pour out your mercy upon us.
Christ, Rising Sun, warm us with your rays,

—and restrain us from every evil impulse.
Keep guard over our thoughts, words and
    actions,
—and make us pleasing in your sight this day.
Turn your gaze from our sinfulness,
—and cleanse us from our iniquities.
Through your cross and resurrection,
—fill us with the consolation of the Spirit.

Our Father . . .

Prayer

GOD our Father,
    you conquer the darkness of ignorance
by the light of your Word.
Strengthen within our hearts
the faith you have given us;
let not temptation ever quench the fire
that your love has kindled within us.

We ask this through our Lord Jesus Christ, your
    Son,
who lives and reigns with you and the Holy
    Spirit,
one God, for ever and ever.

(Dismissal, p. 141)

FRIDAY EVENING

Reflection

IN PSALM 41 the mind and heart of Jesus
Christ during his passion are opened for us
to see. With words from this psalm Jesus spoke
of his betrayal by Judas (Mark 14:18) and his
deliverance into the hands of enemies who hated
him. At the same time, we see in this psalm his
confidence in the mercy and protection of his
Father.

The forgiveness and patience Jesus Christ offered to his betrayer and those who put him to
death tell of God's mercy to us. Even though we
are sinners, God has made an everlasting covenant of forgiveness with us.

The Lord of hosts is with us:
The God of Jacob is our stronghold.

This evening we celebrate God's mercy revealed in the passion of his Son, and we in turn are
reminded to forgive those around us.

The reading from Romans, recalling the patient endurance of Jesus Christ, urges that "we
who are strong in faith should be patient with
the scruples of those whose faith is weak."

EVENING PRAYER

GOD, come to my assistance.
— Lord, make haste to help me.
Glory to the Father, and to the Son, and to the
Holy Spirit:
— as it was in the beginning, is now, and will be
for ever. Amen. Alleluia.

Hymn no 23 or see Guide, 348.

Lord, lay your heal-ing hand up - on —— me;

for I have sinned

Psalm 41

Prayer of a sick person

*One of you will betray me, yes, one who eats with
me* (Mark 14:18).

HAPPY the man who considers the poor
and the weak.
The Lord will save him in the day of evil,
will guard him, give him life, make him happy in the land
and will not give him up to the will of his
foes.
The Lord will help him on his bed of pain,
he will bring him back from sickness to
health.
As for me, I said: "Lord, have mercy on me,

heal my soul for I have sinned against you."
My foes are speaking evil against me.
"How long before he dies and his name be
   forgotten?"
They come to visit me and speak empty
   words,
their hearts full of malice, they spread it
   abroad.

My enemies whisper together against me.
They all weigh up the evil which is on me:
"Some deadly thing has fastened upon him,
he will not rise again from where he lies."
Thus even my friend, in whom I trusted,
who ate my bread, has turned against me.

But you, O Lord, have mercy on me.
Let me rise once more and I will repay them.
By this I shall know that you are my friend,
if my foes do not shout in triumph over me.
If you uphold me I shall be unharmed
and set in your presence for evermore.

Blessed be the Lord, the God of Israel
from age to age. Amen. Amen.

Glory to the Father, and to the Son, and to the
   Holy Spirit:
as it was in the beginning, is now, and will be
   for ever. Amen.

Psalm-prayer

   Lord Jesus, healer of soul and body, you said:
Blessed are the merciful, they will obtain mercy.
Teach us to come to the aid of the needy in a
spirit of brotherly love, that we in turn may be
received and strengthened by you.

The might-y Lord is with us, the God of Ja-cob is our strong-hold.

Psalm 46

God our refuge and strength

He shall be called Emmanuel, which means: God-with-us (Matthew 1:23).

GOD is for us a refuge and strength,
    a helper close at hand, in time of distress:
so we shall not fear though the earth should rock,
though the mountains fall into the depths of the sea,
even though its waters rage and foam,
even though the mountains be shaken by its waves.

The Lord of hosts is with us:
the God of Jacob is our stronghold.

The waters of a river give joy to God's city,
the holy place where the Most High dwells.
God is within, it cannot be shaken;
God will help it at the dawning of the day.
Nations are in tumult, kingdoms are shaken:
he lifts his voice, the earth shrinks away.

The Lord of hosts is with us:
the God of Jacob is our stronghold.

Come, consider the works of the Lord,
the redoubtable deeds he has done on the
earth.
He puts an end to wars over all the earth;
the bow he breaks, the spear he snaps.
He burns the shields with fire.
"Be still and know that I am God,
supreme among the nations, supreme on the
earth!"

The Lord of hosts is with us:
the God of Jacob is our stronghold.

Glory to the Father, and to the Son, and to the
Holy Spirit:
as it was in the beginning, is now, and will be
for ever. Amen.

Psalm-prayer

All-powerful Father, the refuge and strength
of your people, you protect in adversity and defend in prosperity those who put their trust in
you. May they persevere in seeking your will
and find their way to you through obedience.

All na-tions will come and wor-ship
be-fore you, O Lord.

Canticle: Revelation 15:3-4

Hymn of adoration

MIGHTY and wonderful are your works,
Lord God Almighty!
Righteous and true are your ways,
O King of the nations!

Who would dare refuse you honor,
or the glory due your name, O Lord?

Since you alone are holy,
all nations shall come
and worship in your presence.
Your mighty deeds are clearly seen.

Glory to the Father, and to the Son, and to the
Holy Spirit:
as it was in the beginning, is now, and will be
for ever. Amen.

Reading

Romans 15:1-3

WE WHO are strong in faith should be patient
with the scruples of those whose faith is
weak; we must not be selfish. Each should please
his neighbor so as to do him good by building
up his spirit. Thus, in accord with Scripture,
Christ did not please himself: "The reproaches
they uttered against you fell on me."

Responsory

Christ loved us and washed away our sins, in his
own blood.
—Christ loved us and washed away our sins, in
his own blood.

He made us a nation of kings and priests,
— in his own blood.
Glory to the Father . . .
— Christ loved us . . .

Canticle of Mary

Ant.   The Lord has come to the help of his
        servants, for he has remembered his
        promise of mercy.

(Turn to p. 131)

Intercessions

BLESSED be God, who hears the prayers of
the needy, and fills the hungry with good
things. Let us pray to him in confidence:
Lord, show us your mercy.
Merciful Father, upon the cross Jesus offered
you the perfect evening sacrifice,
— we pray now for all the suffering members of
his Church.
Release those in bondage, give sight to the blind,
— shelter the widow and the orphan.
Clothe your faithful people in the armor of salvation,
— and shield them from the deceptions of the
devil.
Let your merciful presence be with us, Lord, at
the hour of our death,
— may we be found faithful and leave this world
in your peace.
Lead the departed into the light of your dwelling-
place,
— that they may gaze upon you for all eternity.
Our Father . . .

Prayer

GOD our Father,
help us to follow the example
of your Son's patience in suffering.
By sharing the burden he carries,
may we come to share his glory
in the kingdom where he lives with you and the
    Holy Spirit,
one God, for ever and ever.

(Turn to p. 141)

SATURDAY MORNING

Reflection

AN ANCIENT song of deliverance—the Canticle of Moses—stands at the center of this morning's prayer. Safely over the Red Sea and freed from the grip of Pharaoh's slavery in Egypt, Moses lifts his voice in praise of the mercy and power of God.

Delivered from the darkness of sin through Christ and re-created through the life-giving waters of baptism; the Christian sings this same song. God has redeemed us and guides us to his holy dwelling.

The promise of God, made long ago to his chosen people as he led them to salvation, is extended now to all nations. His love and faithfulness is offered to all (Psalm 117).

God's goodness, however, always waits for our response and acceptance.

MORNING PRAYER

LORD, open my lips.
— And my mouth will proclaim your praise.

Glory to, etc.:   — as it was, etc.

Ant.   Come, let us worship God who holds the world and its wonders in his creating hand.

Invitatory psalm, p 128.

Hymn no. 22 or see Guide, 348.

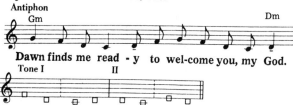

Antiphon

Dawn finds me read - y to wel-come you, my God.

Tone I   II

Psalm 119:145-152
XIX (Koph)

I CALL with all my heart; Lord, hear me,
I will keep your commands.
I call upon you, save me
and I will do your will.

I rise before dawn and cry for help,
I hope in your word.
My eyes watch through the night
to ponder your promise.

In your love hear my voice, O Lord:
give me life by your decrees.
Those who harm me unjustly draw near:
they are far from your law.

But you, O Lord, are close:
your commands are truth.
Long have I known that your will
is established for ever.

Glory to the Father, and to the Son, and to the
Holy Spirit:
as it was in the beginning, is now, and will be
for ever. Amen.

Psalm-prayer

Save us by the power of your hand, Father, for our enemies have ignored your words. May the fire of your word consume our sins and its brightness illumine our hearts.

Canticle

The Lord is my strength, and I shall sing his praise, for he has be-come my Sav-ior.

Canticle: Exodus 15:1-4a, 8-13, 17-18

Hymn of victory after the crossing of the Red Sea

Those who had conquered the beast were singing the song of Moses, God's servant (see Revelation 15:2-3).

I WILL sing to the Lord, for he is gloriously triumphant;
horse and chariot he has cast into the sea.

My strength and my courage is the Lord,
and he has been my savior.
He is my God, I praise him;
the God of my father, I extol him.

The Lord is a warrior,
Lord is his name!
Pharaoh's chariots and army he hurled into the sea.

At a breath of your anger the waters piled
up,
the flowing waters stood like a mound,
the flood waters congealed in the midst of
the sea.

The enemy boasted, "I will pursue and overtake them;
I will divide the spoils and have my fill of
them;
I will draw my sword; my hand shall despoil
them!"
When your wind blew, the sea covered them;
like lead they sank in the mighty waters.

Who is like to you among the gods, O Lord?
Who is like to you, magnificent in holiness?
O terrible in renown, worker of wonders,
when you stretched out your right hand, the
earth swallowed them!

In your mercy you led the people you redeemed;
in your strength you guided them to your
holy dwelling.

And you brought them in and planted them
on the mountain of your inheritance—
the place where you made your seat, O Lord,
the sanctuary, O Lord, which your hands
established.
The Lord shall reign forever and ever.

Glory to the Father, and to the Son, and to the
Holy Spirit:
as it was in the beginning, is now, and will be
for ever. Amen.

Antiphon

O praise the Lord, all you na - tions.

Tone I   II

Psalm 117

Praise for God's loving compassion

I affirm that ... the Gentile peoples are to praise God because of his mercy (Romans 15:8-9).

O PRAISE the Lord, all you nations,
acclaim him, all you peoples!

Strong is his love for us;
he is faithful for ever.

Glory to the Father, and to the Son, and to the
Holy Spirit:
as it was in the beginning, is now, and will be
for ever. Amen.

Psalm-prayer

God our Father, may all nations and peoples
praise you. May Jesus, who is called faithful and
true and who lives with you eternally, possess
our hearts for ever.

Reading

2 Peter 1:10-11

BE SOLICITOUS to make your call and elec-
tion permanent, brothers; surely those who

do so will never be lost. On the contrary, your entry into the everlasting kingdom of our Lord and Savior Jesus Christ will be richly provided for.

Responsory

I cry to you, O Lord, for you are my refuge.
— I cry to you, O Lord, for you are my refuge.
You are all I desire in the land of the living;
— for you are my refuge.
Glory to the Father . . .
— I cry to . . .

Canticle of Zechariah

Ant.   Lord, shine on those who dwell in darkness and the shadow of death.

(Turn to p. 130)

Intercessions

L ET us all praise Christ. In order to become our faithful and merciful high priest before the Father's throne, he chose to become one of us, a brother in all things. In prayer we ask of him:
Lord, share with us the treasure of your love.
Sun of Justice, you filled us with light at our baptism,
— we dedicate this day to you.
At every hour of the day, we give you glory,
— in all our deeds, we offer you praise.
Mary, your mother, was obedient to your word,
— direct our lives in accordance with that word.
Our lives are surrounded with passing things; set our hearts on things of heaven,

—so that through faith, hope and charity we may come to enjoy the vision of your glory.

Our Father . . .

Prayer

L ORD,
free us from the dark night of death.
Let the light of resurrection
dawn within our hearts
to bring us to the radiance of eternal life.

We ask this through our Lord Jesus Christ, your Son,
who lives and reigns with you and the Holy Spirit,
one God, for ever and ever.

(Dismissal, p. 141)

COMMON PRAYERS

INVITATORY PSALM

Psalm 95

A call to praise God

Encourage each other while it is still today (Hebrews 3:13)

(The antiphon is recited and then repeated)

COME, let us sing to the Lord
and shout with joy to the Rock who saves us.
Let us approach him with praise and thanksgiving
and sing joyful songs to the Lord.

(Antiphon repeated)

The Lord is God, the mighty God,
the great king over all the gods.
He holds in his hands the depths of the earth
and the highest mountains as well.
He made the sea; it belongs to him,
the dry land, too, for it was formed by his hands.

(Antiphon repeated)

Come, then, let us bow down and worship,
   bending the knee before the Lord, our maker.
For he is our God and we are his people,
   the flock he shepherds.

(Antiphon repeated)

Today, listen to the voice of the Lord:
Do not grow stubborn, as your fathers did
   in the wilderness,
when at Meriba and Massah
   they challenged me and provoked me,
Although they had seen all of my works.

(Antiphon repeated)

Forty years I endured that generation.
I said, "They are a people whose hearts go astray
   and they do not know my ways."
So I swore in my anger,
   "They shall not enter into my rest."

(Antiphon repeated)

Glory to the Father, and to the Son, and to the
   Holy Spirit:
as it was in the beginning, is now, and will be
   for ever. Amen.

(Antiphon repeated)

In individual recitation, the antiphon may be said only at the beginning of the psalm; it need not be repeated after each strophe.

For psalm 95 one may substitute psalm 100, 67, or 24. If any of these psalms should occur in the office, psalm 95 is then said in place of it.

The psalm with its antiphon may be omitted when the invitatory precedes Morning Prayer.

Canticle of Zechariah

The Messiah and his forerunner

BLESSED be the Lord, the God of Israel;
he has come to his people and / set them free.

He has raised up for us a mighty savior,
born of the house of his / servant David.

Through his holy prophets he promised of old
 that he would save us from our enemies,
 from the hands of / all who hate us.

He promised to show mercy to our fathers
and to remember his / holy covenant.

This was the oath he swore to our father Abraham:
to set us free from the hands / of our enemies,
free to worship him without fear,
holy and righteous in his sight
 all the days / of our life.

You, my child, shall be called the prophet of the
 Most High;
for you will go before the Lord to pre / pare his
 way,
to give his people knowledge of salvation
by the forgiveness / of their sins.

In the tender compassion of our God
the dawn from on high shall break upon us,
to shine on those who dwell in darkness and the
 shadow of death,
and to guide our feet into the / way of peace.
Glory to the Father, etc.

Canticle of Mary

The soul rejoices in the Lord

MY SOUL proclaims the greatness of the Lord,
my spirit rejoices in God my Savior
for he has looked with favor on his lowly servant.

From this day all generations will call me blessed:
the Almighty has done great things for me,
and holy is his Name.

He has mercy on those who fear him
in every generation.

He has shown the strength of his arm,
he has scattered the proud in their conceit.

He has cast down the mighty from their thrones,
and has lifted up the lowly.

He has filled the hungry with good things
and the rich he has sent away empty.

He has come to the help of his servant Israel
for he has remembered his promise of mercy,
the promise he made to our fathers,
to Abraham and his children for ever.

Glory to the Father, etc.

(Music, p. 368)

CONCLUDING PRAYERS FOR THE SEASONS

Advent

Opening Prayer, 1st Sun.

ALL-POWERFUL God,
increase our strength of will for doing good
that Christ may find an eager welcome at his
coming
and call us to his side in the kingdom of heaven,
where he lives and reigns with you and the Holy
Spirit,
one God, for ever and ever.

Alternative Prayer

Father in heaven,
our hearts desire the warmth of your love
and our minds are searching for the light of your
Word.

Increase our longing for Christ our Savior
and give us the strength to grow in love,
that the dawn of his coming
may find us rejoicing in his presence
and welcoming the light of his truth.

We ask this in the name of Jesus the Lord.

Christmas

Opening Prayer, 2nd Sun.

GOD of power and life,
glory of all who believe in you,
fill the world with your splendor

and show the nations the light of your truth.

We ask this through our Lord Jesus Christ, your
    Son,
who lives and reigns with you and the Holy Spirit,
one God, for ever and ever.

Alternative Prayer

Father of our Lord Jesus Christ,
our glory is to stand before the world
as your own sons and daughters.
May the simple beauty of Jesus' birth
summon us always to love what is most deeply
    human,
and to see your Word made flesh
reflected in those whose lives we touch.

We ask this through Christ our Lord.

Lent

Opening Prayer, 1st Sun.

FATHER,
    through our observance of Lent,
help us to understand the meaning
of your Son's death and resurrection,
and teach us to reflect it in our lives.

Grant this through our Lord Jesus Christ, your
    Son,
who lives and reigns with you and the Holy Spirit,
one God, for ever and ever.

Alternative Prayer

Lord our God,
you formed man from the clay of the earth
and breathed into him the spirit of life,
but he turned from your face and sinned.

In this time of repentance
we call out for your mercy.
Bring us back to you
and to the life your Son won for us
by his death on the cross,
for he lives and reigns for ever and ever.

Easter

Opening Prayer, 2nd Sun.

GOD of mercy,
you wash away our sins in water,
you give us new birth in the Spirit,
and redeem us in the blood of Christ.
As we celebrate Christ's resurrection
increase our awareness of these blessings,
and renew your gift of life within us.

We ask this through our Lord Jesus Christ, your
    Son,
who lives and reigns with you and the Holy Spirit,
one God, for ever and ever.

Alternative Prayer

Heavenly Father and God of mercy,
we no longer look for Jesus among the dead,
for he is alive and has become the Lord of life.
From the waters of death you raise us with him
and renew your gift of life within us.

Increase in our minds and hearts
the risen life we share with Christ
and help us to grow as your people
toward the fullness of eternal life with you.
We ask this through Christ our Lord.

Pentecost

Opening Prayer, Pentecost Sun.

GOD our Father,
let the Spirit you sent on your Church
to begin the teaching of the gospel
continue to work in the world
through the hearts of all who believe.
We ask this through our Lord Jesus Christ, your
   Son,
who lives and reigns . . . for ever and ever.

Alternative Prayer

Father of light, from whom every good gift
   comes,
send your Spirit into our lives
with the power of a mighty wind,
and by the flame of your wisdom
open the horizons of our minds.

Loosen our tongues to sing your praise
in words beyond the power of speech,
for without your Spirit
man could never raise his voice in words of peace
or announce the truth that Jesus is Lord,
who lives and reigns . . . for ever and ever.

Ordinary Time

Opening Prayer, 17th Sun. Ord. Time

GOD our Father and protector,
without you nothing is holy,
nothing has value.
Guide us to everlasting life
by helping us to use wisely
the blessings you have given to the world.

We ask this through our Lord Jesus Christ, your
   Son,
who lives and reigns . . . for ever and ever.

Alternative Prayer

God our Father,
open our eyes to see your hand at work
in the splendor of creation,
in the beauty of human life.
Touched by your hand our world is holy.
Help us to cherish the gifts that surround us,
to share your blessings with our brothers and
   sisters,
and to experience the joy of life in your presence.
We ask this through Christ our Lord.

Opening Prayer, 32nd Sun. Ord. Time

GOD of power and mercy,
   protect us from all harm.
Give us freedom of spirit
and health in mind and body
to do your work on earth.

We ask this through our Lord Jesus Christ, your
   Son,
who lives and reigns . . . for ever and ever.

Alternative Prayer

Almighty Father,
strong is your justice and great is your mercy.
Protect us in the burdens and challenges of life.
Shield our minds from the distortion of pride
and enfold our desire with the beauty of truth.

Help us to become more aware of your loving
   design

so that we may more willingly give our lives in
   service to all.
We ask this through Christ our Lord.

Opening Prayer, 5th Sun. Ord. Time

FATHER
   watch over your family
and keep us safe in your care,
for all our hope is in you.
Grant this through our Lord Jesus Christ, your
   Son,
who lives and reigns with you and the Holy Spirit,
one God, for ever and ever.

Alternative Prayer

In faith and love we ask you, Father,
to watch over your family gathered here.
In your mercy and loving kindness
no thought of ours is left unguarded,
no tear unheeded, no joy unnoticed.

Through the prayer of Jesus
may the blessings promised to the poor in spirit
lead us to the treasures of your heavenly kingdom.

We ask this in the name of Jesus the Lord.

Opening Prayer, 7th Sun. Ord. Time

FATHER,
   keep before us the wisdom and love
you have revealed in your Son.
Help us to be like him
in word and deed,
for he lives and reigns . . . for ever and ever.

Alternative Prayer

Almighty God,
Father of our Lord Jesus Christ,
faith in your word is the way to wisdom,
and to ponder your divine plan is to grow in the
    truth.

Open our eyes to your deeds,
our ears to the sound of your call,
so that our every act may increase our sharing
in the life you have offered us.
Grant this through Christ our Lord.

Opening Prayer, 26th Sun. Ord. Time

FATHER, you show your almighty power
    in your mercy and forgiveness.
Continue to fill us with your gifts of love.
Help us to hurry toward the eternal life you
    promise
and come to share in the joys of your kingdom.
Grant this through our Lord Jesus Christ, your
    Son,
who lives and reigns with you and the Holy Spirit,
one God, for ever and ever.

Alternative Prayer

Father of our Lord Jesus Christ,
in your unbounded mercy
you have revealed the beauty of your power
through your constant forgiveness of our sins.

May the power of this love be in our hearts
to bring your pardon and your kingdom to all we
    meet.
We ask this through Christ our Lord.

CONCLUDING PRAYERS
FOR THE SAINTS

Mary, the Mother of God
Opening Prayer, Comm. of BVM

Lord Jesus Christ,
you chose the Virgin Mary to be your mother,
a worthy home in which to dwell.
By her prayers keep us from danger
and bring us to the joy of heaven,
where you live and reign with the Father and
the Holy Spirit, one God, for ever and ever.

The Apostles
Opening Prayer, Votive Mass of Apostles

Lord,
give your Church the constant joy of honoring
the holy apostles.
May we continue to be guided and governed by
those leaders
whose teaching and example have been our
inspiration.
We ask this through our Lord Jesus Christ,
your Son,
who lives and reigns with you and the Holy
Spirit, one God, for ever and ever.

The Martyrs
Opening Prayer, Votive Mass of Martyrs

Lord,
may the victory of your martyrs give us joy.
May their example strengthen our faith,

and their prayers give us renewed courage.

We ask this through our Lord Jesus Christ, your
    Son,
who lives and reigns with you and the Holy
    Spirit, one God, for ever and ever.

All Saints
Opening Prayer, Votive Mass of Saints

God of all holiness,
you gave your saints
different gifts on earth
but one reward in heaven.
May their prayers be our constant encourage-
    ment
for each of us to walk worthily in our vocation.

We ask this through our Lord Jesus Christ,
    your Son,
who lives and reigns with you and the Holy
    Spirit, one God, for ever and ever.

The Angels
Opening Prayer, Votive Mass or Angels

God our Father,
in a wonderful way you guide and govern the
    work of angels and men.
May those who serve you constantly in heaven
keep our lives safe and sure on earth.

We ask this through our Lord Jesus Christ, your
    Son,
who lives and reigns with you and the Holy
    Spirit,
one God, for ever and ever.

Prayer for the Dead
Opening Prayer, Mass for the Dead

God, our creator and redeemer,
by your power Christ conquered death
and returned to you in glory.
May all your people who have gone before us
   in faith share his victory
and enjoy the vision of your glory for ever,
where Christ lives and reigns with you and the
   Holy Spirit,
one God, for ever and ever.

Dismissal

If a priest or deacon presides, he dismisses the people:

The Lord be with you.
— And also with you.

May almighty God bless you,
the Father, and the Son, and the Holy Spirit.
— Amen.

Another form of the blessing may be used, as at Mass.

Then he adds:

Go in peace.
— Thanks be to God.

In the absence of a priest or deacon and in individual
recitation, the Prayer concludes:

May the Lord bless us,
protect us from all evil
and bring us to everlasting life.
— Amen.

"The spiritual life is not confined to participation in the liturgy. The Christian is assuredly called to pray with his brethren, but he must also enter into his chamber to pray to the Father in secret (cf. Matthew 6:6); indeed, according to the teaching of the Apostle Paul, he should pray without ceasing (cf. 1 Thessalonians 5:17)" (Vatican II: Constitution on the Sacred Liturgy, no. 12.)

EXPLORING THE WAYS
OF PRAYER

PRAYER is a conversation with God. And like every conversation, prayer takes many different forms. In fact, it's impossible to describe all the ways people pray.

An ancient monk, Saint Isaac, once said: "There are as many kinds of prayer as there are different states of soul, as many kinds of prayer as there are souls."

We pray as we speak — in distinct voices. Our many-sided personalities, our different human and spiritual gifts, our own experience give the way we pray its own particular intonation.

How do you pray? A brief summary of some ways of praying may help you become aware of your own methods of prayer, and assist you to develop the gifts of prayer God has given you.

The Prayer of the Tax-Collector

Some ways of prayer are extraordinarily simple. Remember, for example, the prayer of the tax-collector that Jesus Christ describes (Luke 18:13-14). He just stood before God, head bowed, striking his breast and repeating a few heartfelt words: "O God, be merciful to me a sinner."

That prayer, pleasing to God, seems so easy to imitate—until we try to make it our own!

Undoubtedly, our best prayers will be like his prayer, coming from our hearts and expressed in simple words and gestures.

Prayer and the Body

As the tax-collector's prayer indicates, we can pray using our bodies—standing, bowing our heads, striking our breasts. We may hardly be aware of it, but all our physical and intellectual powers—our eyes, ears, memories, imagination, intellect and will—provide us with an endless variety of ways to pray.

One ancient prayer technique involving the body uses the ordinary act of breathing:

> You know how we breathe the air in and out. On this is based the life of the body and its warmth. So, sitting in your room, collect your mind, lead it into the path of the breath along with the air and enter in. Go into your heart and stay there. But do not be silent or idle within. Say: "Lord Jesus Christ, Son of God, have mercy on me." Keep saying this prayer.
>
> *(Saint Nicephorus)*

Breathing isn't the only way our bodies can enter the action of prayer. Other ordinary actions like walking, standing, sitting, seeing and listening can become expressions of prayer when done in a spirit of faith.

Try, for example, to walk to a church as a pilgrim seeking God. Let your walking itself be an expression of your pilgrimage, of your desire to enter God's presence.

More complex bodily activities, too, can be prayerful. David danced for joy before the Ark of God, and who will say his dance was not a prayer?

When our bodies enter the act of prayer, we are more likely, at least initially, to pray with greater concentration. For prayer is best made when it involves the whole person.

"Be Still, and Know That I Am God"

Prayer, too, involves silence. Like every conversation, praying requires that we listen, and listening means to be still.

First of all, unnecessary noise within ourselves must be quieted. Because of inner tension, anxiety, or pride, our thoughts can be absorbed in a multitude of personal concerns, making us one-sided conversationalists, preoccupied solely with our own interests.

"The first work of silence," says Saint John Climacus, "is freedom from cares." Our excessive self-concern must be silenced, our faculties must be stilled; otherwise, we remain too busy for God, who is worthy of all our attention.

Prayer requires a climate of silence within and without for being attentive to God. Physical silence can contribute to the deeper silence of the heart. A quiet church or room, a quiet time of the day, a solitary beach or garden can help us meet our Lord and God.

Praying with Your Eyes

The psalmist, proclaiming "The heavens declare the glory of God," prayed from what he saw. Before any words, his eyes were taken up with the wonders of the heavens where they rested in praise. Seeing, he prayed.

Our eyes, too, are blessed when they can see deeply like this.

> To see a World in a Grain of Sand,
> And a Heaven in a Wild Flower,
> Hold Infinity in the palm of your hand,
> And Eternity in an hour.

> *(William Blake)*

That's the way Jesus Christ saw things. The birds of the air, the lilies of the field, salt, seed, the sowing of the fields, trees, water, bread and wine, even the cross—seemingly so devoid of meaning—spoke to him of life's deepest meaning.

Why don't we see things this way, prayerfully and reflectively? Maybe we don't take the time, or perhaps life loses its mystery as we get used to it.

In his tale of childlike wisdom, "The Little Prince," Antoine de Saint Exupery records this sensitive dialogue:

"The men where you live," said the little prince, "raise five thousand roses in the same garden—and they do not find in it what they are looking for."

"They do not find it," I replied.

"And yet what they are looking for could be found in a single rose, or in a little water."

"Yes, that is true," I said.

And the little prince added:

"But the eyes are blind. One must look with the heart."

Once you begin looking at things with your heart, you don't have to look far for the wayside sacraments that lead to the mystery of God. They are before you everywhere.

Look carefully at your own hand, for instance. Do you see how marvelously it has been fashioned! What things you do with that single part of your body! And where did the hand come from?

Or pick up something small, like a rock or a flower, and study its color, its shape and design. It can point to the One who, in the beginning, made heaven and earth.

"The forms of created things are, as it were, their voices praising their creator," says Saint Augustine. They are wayside sacraments. Mountains and hills, busy streets and silent rows of buildings, the thousand faces of young and old, praise God. A beautiful church, a quiet place in our own homes, a restful garden or park, a picture, a plant, a tree can bring visual nourishment and support to our own prayer.

Blessed are our eyes if we can see creation engaged in the praise of its Maker!

What Words Can We Use for Prayer?

Where do you find words for prayer? Look first into your own heart.

"Whenever you pray, go to your room, close your door, and pray to your Father in private," Jesus Christ taught (Matthew 6:6). Pray from your heart, he said, from the depths of your own personality.

Praying from the heart means to speak to God as we truly are, without the masks with which we meet friends or strangers, without our public

roles and countless diversions. It means praying
from our helplessness, frustration, infidelity and
confusion, as well as our love and accomplish-
ments our hopes and our dreams. Only in private,
in the room of our own hearts, can we truly say
"Hear I am, Lord."

Let your heart prompt you when you look for
the words of prayer. And don't be afraid to speak
honest, heartfelt words to God. For God responds
to such prayer. "Then, your Father, who sees
what no man sees, will repay you" (Mt 6:6).

Praying the Words of Holy Scripture

One day Jesus was praying in a certain place.
When he had finished, one of his disciples asked
him, "Lord, teach us to pray. . . .

He said to them, "When you pray, say:
"Father,
hallowed be your name,
your kingdom come.
Give us each day our daily bread.
Forgive us our sins
for we too forgive all who do us wrong;
and subject us not to the trial." (Luke 11:1-4)

Holy Scripture, the Word of God, can provide
us with words of prayer. Nothing is more helpful
to prayer than the frequent reflective reading of
Scripture, where the Spirit of Jesus Christ is present teaching us to pray.

As you read or listen to Scripture, think of it
as God's word to you here and now. Ask yourself
what God wishes in this reading to tell you about

himself and his plan for your life, and how you can respond to him.

The words and deeds of Scripture may challenge or disturb, or set your heart to burning within you with love and confidence. Whatever words or stories particularly inspire you, listen carefully to them. Treasure and ponder them. They are God's special gift.

Reading the Scripture can be done at random, opening it wherever you wish; or according to an ordered plan. For example, you may choose to follow closely the arrangement of scripture readings the Church has made in her Liturgy for various feasts and seasons throughout the year.

Above all, read the Scriptures unhurriedly. "One word was enough to reconcile the thief and the prodigal son to God," says Saint John Climacus. So too. we may find in a few words the promise of paradise or the voice of the Father calling us his own.

Practical Aids for Reading Holy Scripture

Use a good translation when you read Holy Scripture. The best modern translation currently available is:

The New American Bible   (1970)

Where to find. . . .

The Christmas story — Matthew 1, 2; Luke 2

The Passion, Death, and Resurrection of Jesus — Matthew 26-28; Mark 14-16; Luke 22-24; John 13-21.

The Sermon on the Mount — Matthew 5, 6, 7

The Great Commandment — Luke 10:27; Matthew 22:34-40.

The Lord's Prayer — Matthew 6:5-15; Luke 11:1-13.

The Parable of the Prodigal Son — Luke 15

The Parable of the Good Samaritan — Luke 10.

The Teaching on Love — 1 Corinthians 13.

The Good Shepherd Psalm — Psalm 23.

The Ten Commandments — Exodus 30; Deuteronomy 5.

The Mission of the Church — Matthew 28, 19-20; Mark 16, 15.

The Story of Pentecost — Acts 2.

The Last Judgment — Matthew 25.

Praying the Words of Prayer

It may seem obvious, but it's good to recall that prayers help us to pray. They are teachers of prayer.

Along with the great scriptural prayers, like the Lord's Prayer and the psalms, the prayers of the Church and the saints have a proven power to unite us to God. Found in the Liturgy and books of devotion, they have helped countless generations to converse intimately with God.

The "Prayer of Saint Francis" is an example:

Lord, make me an instrument of your peace.
  Where there is hatred, let me sow love;
  Where there is injury, pardon;
  Where there is doubt, faith;
  Where there is despair, hope;
  Where there is darkness, light;
  Where there is sadness, joy.

O Master, grant that I may not so much
  seek to be consoled, as to console;

To be understood, as to understand;
To be loved, as to love;
For it is in giving that we receive;
It is in pardoning that we are pardoned;
And it is in dying that we are born to eternal
    life.

Here again, if you follow the words of these prayers with your heart, they will offer light to the path of your prayer.

Books of prayers and devotions, containing these great prayers, can be useful to you.

Prayer, Music, and Sound

At times, prayer can arise without words, in the music of cymbals, the lyre and harp, according to the psalms. "Awake, lyre and harp, I will wake the dawn" (Psalm 57:9). In many forms, music and sound can enter into the prayer we make to God today.

It may be the steady rhythmic sound that comes while reciting the rosary or a litany. It may be the more complex sounds of music experienced in worship or in our private listening. Sound and music can offer another intonation to the voice of your prayer.

Blessed are our ears, when we hear God's praise in sound!

Praying from Your Memories

Remember.

Repeatedly God urges his people in Holy Scripture to search their own lives for signs of his gracious providence. People throughout history have done this, praying to God out of their memories. Think of the famous "Confessions" of Saint Augustine. Thomas Merton's "Seven Story Mountain" and Dag Hammarskjold's "Markings" are instances from our own day.

Our memories hold a lifetime experience of God's generosity and mercy. His great mysteries of creation and salvation occur, not only in the Bible, but quietly in the normal, everyday circumstances of our lives.

How can you pray from your memories? One way is to prayerfully review each day, for about fifteen minutes, perhaps in the evening before bed, beginning from the present moment, going back to the moment you awakened.

Calmly review the pattern of the day in your mind—your moods, your impressions, your actions, your experiences, your motives. Do this impartially, without praise or blame. Then bring your memories to God for his merciful judgment.

Another way of using memory as a support for prayer is to keep a journal in which you record the patterns of your works, your personal relationships, your inner feelings and thoughts, your dreams, events in society, and your relationship to God.

Prayer and the Imagination

The imagination, too, offers us a way to pray. Teachers of prayer, like Saints Bonaventure, Ignatius Loyola, and Francis de Sales, advise using the imagination particularly when meditating on the stories of the gospel.

Go into the story, they say, and see, hear, and feel through your imaginative powers the Word made flesh.

Meditations for the Imagination

Gospel stories of the life of Jesus are especially suited for this kind of meditation. For example, the birth of Jesus, miracles such as the raising of Lazarus, the Transfiguration, and especially the events of his Passion, Death, and Resurrection.

It may be helpful to have someone guide you through these meditations, or you may wish to record the meditation yourself on a tape-recorder and play it back while you follow it in meditation.

Go slowly through the steps, pausing frequently to let your imagination follow freely the events of the story.

Two sample meditations follow:

Meditation on the Call of Matthew (Matthew 9)

Take a comfortable position and relax. Let your body relax. Let each part of your body relax.

Begin to be aware of your breathing. Breathe slowly and deeply. Concentrate on your breathing, in and out, in and out.

Enter the world of your imagination, now. Imagine yourself in a room and you are alone. On one side of the room is a door. Go to the door. It is like the cover of a beautiful bible. Open it up and go into the world of the bible.

You are in a lovely meadow. What do you see? What do you hear? How do you feel?

There is a small dirt road going into a town. Take the road and walk into the town.

Before a house, a man is sitting at a desk, counting money. This is Matthew, the tax-collector. Go and stand by his desk. What is he like? What kind of a man is he?

As you stand there someone comes to the desk. It is Jesus. What does he look like?

Jesus says to Matthew "Come, follow me."

How does Matthew react initially to those words?

Finally, you see Matthew get up from the desk and go to the side of Jesus. He has chosen to follow him.

As they go, Jesus turns to you and says "Come, follow me." How do you feel as you hear that invitation?

Imagine yourself at the side of Jesus, experiencing his strength, his wisdom, his peace.

See yourself walking with the Lord on a road. It winds far into the distance, over hills and into dark valleys. Parts of the road are difficult to walk. Some of the road is bathed in beautiful light; some of it in darkness. The road is your life.

You are not walking this road alone, however. Imagine yourself walking with the Lord along the road, sharing its joys and challenges with him. You could almost feel like dancing on that road.

Others walk that road with you. Besides Jesus, there is Matthew, and a host of other people. Whom do you see with you?

Slowly begin to leave this scene on the road. Keep its memory with you, though. Remember your union with the Lord, and with all who walk the road of life.

Meditation on the Cross

Begin using the first few directions on relaxation from the preceding meditation.

Go into the world of your imagination.

See yourself ascending a hill from which you can see everything in the world.

Open your arms and stand in the form of a cross.

Consider all the powers you have in your body:
  your eyes, the years of seeing you have;
  your ears, the years of hearing you have;
  your hands and arms, the years of work and experience you have.

Outstretched, like a cross, you signify all your limitless desires.

You reach for the infinite.

You touch the earth and seek to embrace the heavens, the east and the west.

Outstretched, like a cross, you signify the limits of your life.
  The cross is a sign of your life;
  The cross is a sign of your death.

You cannot embrace the earth or the heavens.

You are limited by your sinfulness,
  your sorrows and your fears.

Look at them and consider them.

But see, the Lord Jesus, the Word, who made the
    universe,
        the Savior, come to redeem us;
    See him ascending the hill from which you
        can see everything in the world.
He opens his arms and becomes one with you;
He opens his arms and becomes one with us all.
With love, he takes you to himself;
He takes your sins and sorrows on to himself;
He takes the sins and sorrows of the world on to
    himself.

Our cross becomes his;
His cross becomes ours.

"I have been crucified with Christ,
and the life I live now is not my own; Christ is
    living in me.
I still live my human life,
but it is a life of faith in the Son of God,
who loved me and gave himself for me." (Gl 2:19)

With Christ, I can open my arms.
Now I can embrace the world that is mine.

Now see yourself coming down from the hill
    from which you can see everything in the
    world.
Come back to the world you know, that you saw
    from the cross.

Music, Imagination and Prayer: A Sample Meditation

Select a piece of quietly cheerful instrumental
music to listen to. For example:

Beethoven, String Quartet in F. Adagio or slow movement

> **Violin Concerto in D. Adagio or slow movement**
> **String Quartet, Op. 95. Last two movements.**
> **String Quartet, Opera 95. Last two movements**

Mahler, Symphony No. 5. Slow movement.

Wagner. Tristan and Isolde. Overture.

Take a comfortable position.

Imagine yourself in a meadow. You are seated. As you listen to the music, concentrate on your feet. Feel the music in your feet.

Concentrate on your legs, chest cavity, arms, fingertips. Let the music fill them.

As you sit in the meadow, filled with music, look up. The Lord comes.

Give your imagination to him, and let him take you and show you the world.

What does the world look like as he takes you? What do you see? What do you feel? How are you dressed?

When you wish, return to the meadow. Is there anything you wish to say to Jesus before you part? Say it.

After he leaves, remain quiet. Listen restfully to the music. Let it leave your body, until you hear it only with your ears.

Remain quiet for a few minutes. Reflect on the images from this meditation.

"Christ conquers! Christ reigns! Christ commands!"

READINGS, PRAYERS, and DEVOTIONS
on the Mysteries of Christ

ADVENT SEASON

Poem: The Incarnation

THEN He summoned an archangel,
  Saint Gabriel: and when he came,
Sent him forth to find a maiden,
  Mary was her name.

Only through her consenting love
Could the mystery be preferred
That the Trinity in human
  Flesh might clothe the Word.

Though the three Persons worked the wonder
It only happened in the One.
So was the Word made incarnation
  In Mary's womb, a son.

So He who only had a Father
Now had a Mother undefiled,
Though not as ordinary maids
  Had she conceived the Child.

By Mary, and with her own flesh
He was clothed in His own frame:
Both Son of God and Son of Man
  Together had one name.

Saint John of the Cross: Translator: Roy Campbell

Announcement of the Birth of Jesus

Luke 1:26-38

IN THE sixth month, the angel Gabriel was sent from God to a town of Galilee named Nazareth, to a virgin betrothed to a man named Joseph, of the house of David. The virgin's name was Mary. Upon arriving, the messenger said to her: "Rejoice, highly favored daughter! The Lord is with you. Blessed are you among women." She was deeply troubled by his words, and wondered what his greeting meant. The messenger went on to say to her: "Do not fear, Mary. You have found favor with God. You shall conceive and bear a son and give him the name Jesus. Great will be his dignity and he will be called Son of the Most High. The Lord God will give him the throne of David his father. He will rule over the house of Jacob forever and his reign will be without end."

Mary said to the angel, "How can this be since I do not know man?" The angel answered her: "The Holy Spirit will come upon you and the power of the Most High will overshadow you; hence, the holy offspring to be born will be called Son of God. Know that Elizabeth your kins-woman has conceived a son in her old age; she who was thought to be sterile is now in her sixth month, for nothing is impossible with God."

Mary said: "I am the maidservant of the Lord. Let it be done to me as you say." With that the angel left her.

God's Word will come to us

Bernard: *Sermons*

WE KNOW that there are three comings of the Lord. The third lies between the other two. It is invisible, while the other two are visible. In the first coming he was seen on earth, dwelling among men; he himself testifies that they saw him and hated him. In the final coming *all flesh will see the salvation of our God* and *they will look on him whom they pierced*. The intermediate coming is a hidden one; in it only the elect see the Lord within their own selves, and they are saved. In his first coming our Lord came in our flesh and in our weakness; in this middle coming he comes in spirit and in power; in the final coming he will be seen in glory and majesty.

Because this coming lies between the other two, it is like a road on which we travel from the first coming to the last. In the first, Christ was our redemption; in the last, he will appear as our life; in this middle coming, he is our rest and consolation.

In case someone should think that what we say about this middle coming is sheer invention, listen to what our Lord himself says: *If anyone loves me, he will keep my word, and my Father will love him, and we will come to him.* There is another passage of Scripture which reads: *He who fears God will do good,* but something further has been said about the one who loves, that is, that he will keep God's word. Where is God's word to be kept? Obviously in the heart, as the prophet says: *I have hidden your words in my heart, so that I may not sin against you.*

Keep God's word in this way. Let it enter into your very being, let it take possession of your desires and your whole way of life. Feed on goodness, and your soul will delight in its richness. Remember to eat your bread, or your heart will wither away. Fill your soul with richness and strength.

Prayer

FATHER in heaven,
   our hearts desire the warmth of your love
and our minds are searching for the light of your
   Word.
Increase our longing for Christ our Savior
and give us the strength to grow in love,
that the dawn of his coming
may find us rejoicing in his presence
and welcoming the light of his truth.
We ask this in the name of Jesus the Lord.

(Opening Prayer, 1st Sun. of Advent)

CHRISTMAS SEASON

Poem: In the bleak mid-winter

IN THE bleak mid-winter
  A stable-place sufficed
The Lord God Almighty
  Jesus Christ.

Enough for him, whom cherubim
  Worship night and day,
A breastful of milk
  And a mangerful of hay;
Enough for him, whom angels
  Fall down before,
The ox and ass and camel
  Which adore.

Angels and archangels
  May have gathered there;
Cherubim and Seraphim
  Thronged the air;
But only His mother
  In her maiden bliss
Worshipped the beloved
  With a kiss.

What can I give him,
  Poor as I am?
If I were a shepherd
  I would bring a lamb,
If I were a Wise Man
  I would do my part,
Yet what I can give Him,
  Give my heart.   *Christina Rossetti*

"Mary gave birth to her firstborn son and
wrapped him in swaddling clothes."

Birth of Jesus

Luke 2:1-14

IN THOSE days Caesar Augustus published a decree ordering a census of the whole world. This first census took place while Quirinius was governor of Syria. Everyone went to register, each to his own town. And so Joseph went from the town of Nazareth in Galilee to Judea, to David's town of Bethlehem—because he was of the house and lineage of David—to register with Mary, his espoused wife, who was with child.

While they were there the days of her confinement were completed. She gave birth to her firstborn son and wrapped him in swaddling clothes and laid him in a manger, because there was no room for them in the place where travelers lodged.

There were shepherds in the locality, living in the fields and keeping night watch by turns over their flock. The angel of the Lord appeared to them, as the glory of the Lord shone around them, and they were very much afraid. The angel said to them: "You have nothing to fear! I come to proclaim good news to you—tidings of great joy to be shared by the whole people. This day in David's city a savior has been born to you: in a manger you will find an infant wrapped in swaddling clothes." Suddenly, there was with the angel a multitude of the heavenly host, praising God and saying,

"Glory to God in high heaven,
peace on earth to those on whom his favor rests."

Christian, remember your dignity

Leo the Great: *Sermon*

DEARLY beloved, today our Savior is born; let us rejoice. Sadness should have no place on the birthday of life. The fear of death has been swallowed up; life brings us joy with the promise of eternal happiness.

No one is shut out from this joy; all share the same reason for rejoicing. Our Lord, victor over sin and death, finding no man free from sin, came to free us all. Let the saint rejoice as he sees the palm of victory at hand. Let the sinner be glad as he receives the offer of forgiveness. Let the pagan take courage as he is summoned to life.

In the fullness of time, chosen in the unfathomable depths of God's wisdom, the Son of God took for himself our common humanity in order to reconcile it with its creator. He came to overthrow the devil, the origin of death, in that very nature by which he had overthrown mankind.

And so at the birth of our Lord the angels sing in joy: *Glory to God in the highest,* and they proclaim *peace to his people on earth* as they see the heavenly Jerusalem being built from all the nations of the world. When the angels on high are so exultant at this marvelous work of God's goodness, what joy should it not bring to the lowly hearts of men?

Beloved, let us give thanks to God the Father, through his Son, in the Holy Spirit, because in his great love for us he took pity on us, *and when we were dead in our sins he brought us to life with Christ,* so that in him we might be a new creation. Let us throw off our old nature and all its ways and, as we have come to birth in Christ, let us renounce the works of the flesh.

Christian, remember your dignity, and now that you share in God's own nature, do not return by sin to your former base condition. Bear in mind who is your head and of whose body you are a member. Do not forget that you have been rescued from the power of darkness and brought into the light of God's kingdom.

Through the sacrament of baptism you have become a temple of the Holy Spirit. Do not drive away so great a guest by evil conduct and become again a slave to the devil, for your liberty was bought by the blood of Christ.

Prayer

GOD of love, Father of all,
    the darkness that covered the earth
has given way to the bright dawn of your Word
    made flesh.
Make us a people of this light.
Make us faithful to your Word,
that we may bring your life to the waiting world.
Grant this through Christ our Lord.

(Opening Prayer, Christmas Day)

Circumcision of Jesus

Luke 2:16-21

THE shepherds went in haste to Bethlehem and found Mary and Joseph, and the baby lying in the manger; once they saw, they understood what had been told them concerning this child. All who heard of it were astonished at the report given them by the shepherds.

Mary treasured all these things and reflected on them in her heart. The shepherds returned, glorifying and praising God for all they had heard and seen, in accord with what had been told them.

When the eighth day arrived for his circumcision, the name Jesus was given the child, the name the angel had given him before he was conceived.

Prayer

FATHER,
    source of light in every age,
the virgin conceived and bore your Son
who is called Wonderful God, Prince of Peace.

May her prayer, the gift of a mother's love,
be your people's joy through all ages.
May her response, born of a humble heart,
draw your Spirit to rest on your people.

Grant this through Christ our Lord.

(Opening Prayer, Octave of Christmas)

The astrologers (or magi)

Matthew 2:1-12

AFTER Jesus' birth in Bethlehem of Judea during the reign of King Herod, astrologers from the east arrived one day in Jerusalem inquiring, "Where is the newborn king of the Jews? We observed his star at its rising and have come to pay him homage." At this news King Herod became greatly disturbed, and with him all Jerusalem. Summoning all of the chief priests and scribes of the people, he inquired of them where the Messiah was to be born. "In Bethlehem of Judea," they informed him. "Here is what the prophet has written:

'And you, Bethlehem, land of Judah,
   are by no means least among the princes of
      Judah,
   since from you shall come a ruler
   who is to shepherd my people Israel.' "

Herod called the astrologers aside and found out from them the exact time of the star's appearance. Then he sent them to Bethlehem, after having instructed them: "Go and get detailed information about the child. When you have discovered something, report your findings to me so that I may go and offer him homage too."

After their audience with the king, they set out. The star which they had observed at its rising went ahead of them until it came to a standstill over the place where the child was. They were overjoyed at seeing the star, and on entering the house, found the child with Mary his mother.

They prostrated themselves and did him homage. Then they opened their coffers, and presented him with gifts of gold, frankincense, and myrrh.

They received a message in a dream not to return to Herod, so they went back to their own country by another route.

In choosing to be born for us, God chose to be known by us

Peter Chrysologus: *Sermon*

IN THE mystery of our Lord's incarnation there were clear indications of his eternal Godhead. Yet the great events we celebrate today disclose and reveal in different ways the fact that God himself took a human body. Mortal man, enshrouded always in darkness, must not be left in ignorance, and so be deprived of what he can understand and retain only by grace.

In choosing to be born for us, God chose to be known by us. He therefore reveals himself in this way, in order that this great sacrament of his love may not be an occasion for us of great misunderstanding.

Today the Magi find, crying in a manger, the one they have followed as he shone in the sky. Today the Magi see clearly, in swaddling clothes, the one they have long awaited as he lay hidden among the stars.

Today the Magi gaze in deep wonder at what they see: heaven on earth, earth in heaven, man in God, God in man, one whom the whole universe cannot contain now enclosed in a tiny body. As they look, they believe and do not question, as their symbolic gifts bear witness: incense for God, gold for a king, myrrh for one who is to die.

So the Gentiles, who were the last, become the first: the faith of the Magi is the first fruits of the belief of the Gentiles.

Prayer

FATHER of light, unchanging God,
today you reveal to men of faith
the resplendent fact of the Word made flesh:

Your light is strong,
your love is near;
draw us beyond the limits which this world im-
poses,
to the life where your Spirit makes all life complete.

We ask this through Christ our Lord.

(Opening Prayer, Feast of Epiphany)

The finding in the temple

Luke 2:41-52

THE parents of Jesus used to go every year to Jerusalem for the feast of the Passover, and when he was twelve they went up for the celebration as was their custom. As they were returning at the end of the feast, the child Jesus remained behind unknown to his parents. Thinking he was in the party, they continued their journey for a day, looking for him among their relatives and acquaintances.

Not finding him, they returned to Jerusalem in search of him. On the third day they came upon him in the temple sitting in the midst of the teachers, listening to them and asking them questions. All who heard him were amazed at his intelligence and his answers.

When his parents saw him they were astonished, and his mother said to him: "Son, why have you done this to us? You see that your father and I have been searching for you in sorrow." He said to them: "Why did you search for me? Did you not know I had to be in my Father's house?" But they did not grasp what he said to them.

He went down with them then, and came to Nazareth, and was obedient to them. His mother meanwhile kept all these things in memory. Jesus, for his part, progressed steadily in wisdom and age and grace before God and men.

Prayer

FATHER,
   help us to live as the holy family,
united in respect and love.
Bring us to the joy and peace of your eternal home.

Grant this through our Lord Jesus Christ, your Son,
who lives and reigns with you and the Holy Spirit,
one God, for ever and ever.

(Opening Prayer, Feast of the Holy Family)

LENT

Mark 1:12-15

THE Spirit sent Jesus out toward the desert. He stayed in the wasteland forty days, put to the test there by Satan. He was with the wild beasts, and angels waited on him.

After John's arrest, Jesus appeared in Galilee proclaiming God's good news: "This is the time of fulfillment. The reign of God is at hand! Reform your lives and believe in the good news!"

In Christ we suffered temptation, and in him we overcame the devil

Augustine: *Commentary on the Psalms*

OUR pilgrimage on earth cannot be exempt from trial. We progress by means of trial. No one knows himself except through trial, or receives a crown except after victory, or strives except against an enemy or temptations.

The one who cries from the ends of the earth is in anguish, but is not left on his own. Christ chose to foreshadow us, who are his body, by means of his body, in which he has died, risen and ascended into heaven, so that the members of his body may hope to follow where their head has gone before.

He made us one with him when he chose to be tempted by Satan. We have heard in the gospel how the Lord Jesus Christ was tempted by the devil in the wilderness. Certainly Christ was tempted by the devil. In Christ you were tempted, for Christ received his flesh from your nature, but by his own power gained salvation for you; he suffered death in your nature, but by his own power gained life for you; he suffered insults in your nature, but by his own power gained glory for you; therefore, he suffered temptation in your nature, but by his own power gained victory for you.

If in Christ we have been tempted, in him we overcome the devil. Do you think only of Christ's temptations and fail to think of his victory? See yourself as tempted in him, and see yourself as victorious in him.

Prayer

LORD our God,
   you formed man from the clay of the earth
and breathed into him the spirit of life,
but he turned from your face and sinned.

In this time of repentance
we call out for your mercy.
Bring us back to you
and to the life your Son won for us
by his death on the cross,
for he lives and reigns for ever and ever.
(Opening Prayer, 1st Sun. of Lent)

"Lord, by your cross and resurrection, you have set us free. You are the Savior of the world."

THE STATIONS OF THE CROSS

THE Stations of the Cross is an ancient devotion that combines many ways of praying. The prayers, readings and images that follow may assist you to understand what Jesus meant when he said "Take up your cross and follow me."

Let your entire body enter into this journey if you are in a church or shrine where the stations are erected. From station to station, you are walking with Christ step by step. Let your walking become a prayer.

Let your eyes see beyond these images, these printed words to the reality they symbolize, the Son of God on the way to his death. Let your seeing become a prayer.

Let your imagination recreate the things that happened in this sublime drama. Let your imagination become a prayer.

Let your memory, your experience of life find links of relationship between your history and his. Relate your life to his.

Quietly, in the silence, come to join Jesus Christ. . . . "He who is, who was, and is to come."

Some aids to praying the Stations of the Cross with others have also been added.

Communal Celebration of the Stations of the Cross

1. Prelude (organ/guitar, etc.) optional.
2. Procession to the altar.

3. Opening prayer by the leader. *(below)*

4. Opening refrain and hymn sung by all while proceeding to first station.

5. Announcement of station by the leader.

6. Versicle "We adore you, O Christ . . ." sung or recited by leader or cantor.
Response "By your Cross . . ." sung or recited by the congregation.
A melody will be indicated in the first station.

7. Scriptural introduction sung or recited by cantor or another.

8. Meditation recited by leader or others.

9. Closing refrain sung or recited by cantor or leader, repeated by congregation, while proceeding to next station.

10. Stanzas to the melody of "O Sacred Head" may be sung after opening meditation, and after the fourth, the eighth, and twelfth station.

11. After the fourteenth station, a relic of the Cross may be incensed and the congregation blessed, or some other suitable blessing may be used to conclude the service.

Introduction

Lord Jesus Christ,
I come in faith to remember your
Passion and Death.
Let me walk at your side during your
last journey.

Open my mind and
touch my heart
that I may understand how deep is the love
you show us in your final hours.
Help me to see the sufferings of others as a shar-
     ing
in your bitter sorrows.
Make me attentive to the tragedy in their lives
as I gaze on yours.

O my God,
inspire me to follow bravely in your steps,
carrying my own cross after you.
Long ago the prophet spoke these words for you:
"The Lord God has given me
     a well trained tongue,
That I might know how to speak to the weary
     a word that will rouse them" (Isaiah 50:4).
Speak to me, Lord, from your wounds
and your sufferings.
Stir up my tired spirit
to love you.

Hymn:

> O sacred Head surrounded
>   By crown of piercing thorn!
> O bleeding Head, so wounded,
>   Reviled, and put to scorn!
> Death's pallid hue comes o'er you,
>   The glow of life decays,
> Yet angel hosts adore you,
>   And tremble as they gaze.

First Station

Jesus Is Condemned to Death

Cantor: We adore you, O Christ, and we **bless** you.

All: By your Cross you have redeemed the world.

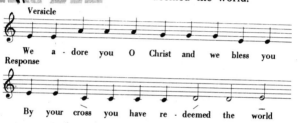

Versicle

We a - dore you O Christ and we bless you

Response

By your cross you have re - deemed the world

Scriptural Introduction

Pilate brought Jesus outside and said to the people, "Look at your king!" At this they shouted, "Away with him! Crucify him!" Then Pilate handed Jesus over to be crucified.

Meditation

Lord Jesus Christ
I believe you are my king, I wish for no other.
Though you stand silently in chains,
you are God,
the Word through whom all things were made,
the Savior sent to redeem us.

As I make my decisions and judgments in life,
let me remember this scene of your judgment.
Give me a sense of true values,
lest I betray what is right, and so betray you.

Guide the choices I make,
however hard they may be,
my King and my Judge.

Closing Refrain:

The Lord is near to all who call on him.

Second Station

Jesus Carries His Cross

Cantor: We adore you, O Christ, and we **bless** you.

All: By your Cross you have redeemed the world.

Scriptural Introduction:

Jesus was led away, and carrying the Cross by himself, went out to what is called the Place of the Skull, Golgotha.

Meditation:

Lord Jesus Christ,
what a strange gift men give you,
this Cross!
How different from the gifts you bring to us,
comfort, healing, encouragement.
Now here is our repayment,
a Cross!
My own return is there also

in that painful burden you bear.
I have been ungrateful for your love.

Lord,
I see you still holding and carrying
a sinful world
in this Cross of yours.
Take me, Lord, sinful and coarse,
and refine my life,
through your redeeming love.

Closing Refrain

O Gód, you arè my **helper, give** me strength

Third Station

Jesus Falls the First Time

Cantor: We adore you, O Christ, and we **bless** you.

All: By your Cross you have redeemed the world.

Scriptural Introduction

Jesus emptied himself, and took the form of a slave, being born in the likeness of men. He humbled himself, to death and a Cross.

Meditation:

Lord Jesus Christ,
how strange a sight to see you, our Mighty God,
stumble and fall.
Weakened by your sufferings and the weight of
    the Cross,
you fall as all men and women do,
when they reach the end of their strength.

Lord,
remember the empty taste of your own weakness,
and be with me when I cannot go on.
You are my hope and my strength,
my rock and my shield.
When I reach the limit of my endurance,
when my heart and body fail,
be with me at my side.

Closing Refrain:

The Lórd is Ròck, and **he** is my salvátion

Fourth Station

Jesus Meets His Mother

Cantor: We adore you, O Christ, and we **bless** you.

All: By your Cross you have re-deemed the world.

Scriptural Introduction

Simeon said to Mary his mother: "This child is destined to be the downfall and the rise of many in Israel, a sign that will be opposed. And you yourself shall be pierced with a sword, so that the thoughts of many hearts will be laid bare."

Meditation:

Lord Jesus Christ,
your meeting with your mother here on the way
to Calvary
is the sword that Simeon foretold
would pierce her heart.

To her, you are not an unfortunate man on the
   way to his death.
You are her son.
She bore you in a stable;
she watched you grow in wisdom and grace,
she took pride in your public life.
Now she must share in the anguish of your death.
Lord,
may I share in your mysteries
together with your mother.
And as I share with you, may you share in all the
   events of my life,
in my joys, my achievements, my sorrows.

Closing Refrain
I móurn with yòu, O **Mary,** Mother of Gód

Hymn
   O Mother of my Savior,
      You stand beside your Son.
   With love beyond all telling,
      You share his grief as one.
   How shall I know your sorrow,
      Your tears beyond compare?
   Deep in my heart stand watching,
      And call my memory there.

Fifth Station

Simon of Cyrene Helps Jesus Bear His Cross

Cantor: We adore you, O Christ,
      and we **bless** you.
All: By your Cross you have re-
      deemed the world.

Scriptural Introduction

A man named Simon of Cyrene, was coming in from the fields, and they pressed him into service to carry the Cross.

Meditation

Lord Jesus Christ,
unlike your mother,
Simon of Cyrene was a passing stranger,
unready and unwilling to share his life with you,
particularly when it meant the social disgrace of
    carrying your Cross.
Did he come to see you as the Light of the World
under your guise of sorrow?
All men and women are meant to.

Lord,
in all places and situations where you offer
to share your Cross with me,
may I remember that the Cross is yours
and you are asking me to share
in the glory of it.
Help me to take it up willingly.

Closing Refrain

I sháll not wànt; my **shepherd** is the Lòrd.

Sixth Station

Veronica Wipes the Face of Jesus

Cantor: We adore you, O Christ, and we **bless** you.

All: By your Cross you have redeemed the world.

Scriptural Introduction

He who welcomes you, welcomes me; and he who welcomes me, welcomes him who sent me. And I promise that whoever gives a cup of cold water will not want for his reward.

Meditation

Lord Jesus Christ,
in compassion Veronica offered you a towel
to wipe the dust and blood and sweat from your
  face.
She dared the contempt and hostility of an ex-
  cited crowd,
for, under your disfigurement,
she discerned the glory
of the Son of God.

Lord,
in the needy and unnoticed
people of this world,
may I see your face
and open my heart to them.

Closing Refrain:

I seék your facè, O **Lord,** and I shall líve

Seventh Station

Jesus Falls the Second Time

Cantor: We adore you, O Christ, and we **bless** you.
All: By your Cross you have redeemed the world.

Scriptural Introduction

But I am a worm, not a man; the scorn of men, despised of the people. All who see me scoff at me.

Meditation

Lord Jesus Christ,
in your miracles you healed
the blind, the lepers, those who were paralyzed.
Now in your passion you experience their darkness,
their misery, their helplessness.
Falling beneath your Cross,
you feel the depths of all human sorrow.

Lord,
may I not run away from human misery
in others and in myself.
Following in your steps,
let me heal when I can
and suffer patiently when I cannot.

Closing Refrain:

O Gód, make hastè to **help** me in my néed

Eighth Station

Jesus Speaks to the Women of Jersalem

Cantor: We adore you, O Christ, and we **bless** you.

All: By your Cross you have redeemed the world.

Scriptural Introduction

A great crowd of people followed him, including women who beat their breasts and lamented over him. Jesus turned to them and said: "Daughters of Jerusalem, do not weep over me. Weep for yourselves and for your children."

Meditation

Lord Jesus Christ,
How surprising to see you
from the depths of your sorrow
reach out and give!
Meeting the sorrowing women,
you think less of yourself than of them.
"Weep not for me, but for your children."
Your Passion is truly a pouring out of yourself
for others!

Lord, may my own troubles and sufferings
not make me unmindful of my neighbor's needs.
Let me support others and give,
even when I myself am in sorrow.

Closing Refrain:

I see thy strength and vigor
All fading in the strife,

And death with cruel rigor
  Bereaving thee of life;
O agony and dying!
  O love to sinners free!
Jesus, all grace supplying,
  O turn thy face to me.

Hymn: A humble heàrt, **O God,** I offer you.

Ninth Station

Jesus Falls the Third Time

All: By your Cross you have redeemed the world.

Cantor: We adore you, O Christ, and we **bless** you.

Scriptural Introduction

I am like water poured out; all my bones are racked. You have brought me down to the dust of death.

Meditation

Lord Jesus Christ,
you refuse to use your Godly power
to prevent your falling a third time.
You lie there helpless,
abandoned even by your disciples.
You had commanded the wind and the sea,
but now you have no human strength
to lift yourself to your feet.

Lord,
in my strength,

let me be aware of my weakness.
In my weakness,
let me have the support of that power
which you refused to use for yourself.
You do not abandon the poor
who hope in your kindness.

Closing Refrain:

O wáit, be stròng; O **wait** before the Lórd.

Tenth Station

Jesus Is Stripped
of His Garments

Cantor: We adore you, O Christ, and we **bless** you.

All: By your Cross you have redeemed the world.

Scriptural Introduction

They stripped off his clothes and began to mock him saying: "All hail, king of the Jews!"

Meditation

Lord Jesus Christ,
now you suffer this new indignity
when the soldiers strip you
of your garments.
As Son of Man with no place to lay your head,
you accepted the poverty of a manger and a
    homeless public life.
Now your very clothing is taken from you
and you are shamed in the eyes of men.
Emptying yourself of all you possessed,

you fulfill your Father's plan for the
coming of his kingdom.

Lord,
seeing you stripped of your garments,
may I repeat with the prophet Job:
"Naked I came forth from my mother's womb
and naked shall I go back again.
The Lord gave and the Lord has taken away,
blessed be the name of the Lord."

Closing Refrain:
I trust in God, I **shall** not be ashamed

Eleventh Station

Jesus Is Nailed to the Cross

Cantor: We adore you, O Christ,
and we **bless** you.

All: By your Cross you have redeemed the world.

Scriptural Introduction

After carrying his Cross, Jesus came to the
Place of the Skull (in Hebrew, Golgotha). There
they crucified him and two others with him.

Meditation

Lord Jesus Christ,
nailed to the Cross and immobilized,
your suffering typifies that which comes to everyone
who experiences life's harsh limitations.
You know the sorrow of everyone bound by poor
health,

by what they might call bad luck,
by family tragedy,
by opposition,
by years and years of getting nowhere.

Lord,
as I feel such nails
limiting my hopes and expectations,
as I experience the Cross
which binds me to what seems like futility,
give me some of your patience
to transform what I endure.

Closing Refrain

To yoú, O Lòrd, I **lift** my soul in práyer

Twelfth Station

Jesus Dies on the Cross

Cantor: We adore you, O Christ, and we **bless** you.

All: By your Cross you have redeemed the world.

Scriptural Introduction:

Jesus said "I thirst!", and they gave him wine.
"It is finished!" he cried, and gave up his spirit.

Meditation

Lord Jesus Christ,
you open your arms on the Cross
and lovingly embrace a sinful world.
You are the Word,
through whom all things were made.

You are the Life whose death
renews everything.
You are the Holy One who take upon yourself
the sins of us all.
You wash the earth clean by your precious Blood.
All men and women from the time of Adam
surround your life-giving Cross
and praise your infinite love.

Lord,
I stand beneath your Cross,
my arms open,
to thank you for offering your life for me.

Closing Refrain

I sháll not diè, O **Lord,** but I shall líve

Hymn

In this, thy bitter passion,
    Good Shepherd, think of me
With thy most sweet compassion,
    Unworthy though I be;
Beneath thy cross abiding
    Forever would I rest,
In thy dear love confiding,
    And with thy presence blest.

Thirteenth Station

Jesus Is Taken Down from the Cross

Cantor: We adore you, O Christ, and we **bless** you.

All: By your Cross you have re- deemed the world.

Scriptural Introduction

When the soldiers came to Jesus and saw that he was already dead, they did not break his legs. But one of the soldiers thrust a lance into his side, and blood and water flowed out. Thus was the Scripture fulfilled: "They shall look on him whom they have pierced."

Meditation

Lord Jesus Christ,
you empty yourself
accepting death
even on a Cross.
Obedient to the Father,
you trust in his goodness
even to the test of death.

Lord,
give me an unfailing trust in your love for me.
Let my last breath
commend my spirit
into the Father's hands.

Closing Refrain

The stóne cast òff be**comes** the cornerstone

Fourteenth Station

Jesus Is Laid in the Tomb

Cantor: We adore you, O Christ, and we **bless** you.

All: By your Cross you have redeemed the world.

Scriptural Introduction

Joseph of Arimathea asked Pilate for the body of Jesus, and wrapped it in perfumed oils. Then he buried Jesus in a tomb close at hand.

Meditation

Lord Jesus,
your friends carry your body for burial to a tomb in a garden.
But you will break the bonds of death
and bless every tomb
with the power and hope of Resurrection.

Lord,
make me rise again
after dying with you.
May all those who have fallen asleep
rise again.

Closing Refrain

I rést in hopè, I **shall** arise from sléep

Hymn

Concluding Blessing

O JESUS, we adore you,
   Our Lord and gracious King.
You bore our sins in sorrow
And brought us healing.
O speak unto my heart, Lord,
As silently you lie.
In death you bring to sinners
The hope of paradise.

Jesus' entry into Jerusalem

John 12:12-16

THE great crowd that had come for the feast heard that Jesus was to enter Jerusalem, so they got palm branches and came out to meet him. They kept shouting:

"Hosanna!

Blessed is he who comes in the name of the Lord!

Blessed is the King of Israel!"

Jesus found a donkey and mounted it, in accord with Scripture:

"Fear not, O daughter of Zion!

Your king approaches you

on a donkey's colt."

(At first, the disciples did not understand all this, but after Jesus was glorified they recalled that the people had done to him precisely what had been written about him.)

Blessed is he who comes in the name
of the Lord. Blessed is the king of Israel.

Andrew of Crete: *Sermon*

LET us go together to meet Christ on the Mount Olives. Today he returns from Bethany and proceeds of his own free will toward his holy and blessed passion, to consummate the mystery of our salvation. He who came down from heaven to raise us from the depths of sin, to raise us with himself, we are told in Scripture, *above every sovereignty, authority and power, and every other name that can be named,* now comes of his own free will to make his journey to Jerusalem. He comes without pomp or ostentation. As the psalmist says: *He will not dispute or raise his voice to make it heard in the streets.* He will be meek and humble, and he will make his entry in simplicity.

Let us run to accompany him as he hastens toward his passion, and imitate those who met him then, not by covering his path with garments, olive branches or palms, but by doing all we can to prostrate ourselves before him by being humble and by trying to live as he would wish. Then we shall be able to receive the Word at his coming, and God, whom no limits can contain, will be within us.

In his humility Christ entered the dark regions of our fallen world and he is glad that he became so humble for our sake, glad that he came and lived among us and shared in our nature in order to raise us up again to himself. And even though we are told that he has now ascended above the highest heavens—the proof, surely, of his power and godhead—his love for man will never rest until he has raised our earthbound nature from glory to glory, and made it one with his own in heaven.

So let us spread before his feet, not garments or soulless olive branches, which delight the eye

ON THE MYSTERIES OF CHRIST

for a few hours and then wither, but ourselves,
clothed in his grace, or rather, clothed completely
in him. We who have been baptized into Christ
must ourselves be the garments that we spread
before him. Now that the crimson stains of our
sins have been washed away in the saving waters
of baptism and we have become white as pure
wool, let us present the conqueror of death, not
with mere branches of palms but with the real
rewards of his victory. Let our souls take the
place of welcoming branches as we join today
in the children's holy song: *Blessed is he who
comes in the name of the Lord. Blessed is the
king of Israel.*

Prayer

ALMIGHTY, ever-living God,
   you have given the human race Jesus Christ
   our Savior
as a model of humility.
He fulfilled your will
by becoming man and giving his life on the cross.
Help us to bear witness to you
by following his example of suffering
and make us worthy to share in his resurrection.

We ask this through our Lord Jesus Christ, your
   Son,
who lives and reigns with you and the Holy Spirit,
one God, for ever and ever.

(Opening Prayer, Passion Sunday)

The Holy Eucharist

Mark 14:12-16, 22-26

ON THE first day of Unleavened Bread, when it was customary to sacrifice the paschal lamb, the disciples said to Jesus, "Where do you wish us to go to prepare the Passover supper for you?" He sent two of his disciples with these instructions: "Go into the city and you will come upon a man carrying a water jar. Follow him. Whatever house he enters, say to the owner, 'The Teacher asks, Where is my guest room where I may eat the Passover with my disciples?' Then he will show you an upstairs room, spacious, furnished, and all in order. That is the place you are to get ready for us." The disciples went off. When they reached the city they found it just as he had told them, and they prepared the Passover supper.

During the meal he took bread, blessed and broke it, and gave it to them. "Take this," he said, "this is my body." He likewise took a cup, gave thanks and passed it to them, and they all drank from it. He said to them: "This is my blood, the blood of the covenant, to be poured out on behalf of many. I solemnly assure you, I will never again drink of the fruit of the vine until the day when I drink it new in the reign of God."

After singing songs of praise they walked out to the Mount of Olives.

O precious and wonderful banquet!

Thomas Aquinas: *Work*

SINCE it was the will of God's only-begotten Son that men should share in his divinity, he assumed our nature in order that by becoming man he might make men gods. Moreover, when he took our flesh he dedicated the whole of its substance to our salvation. He offered his body to God the Father on the altar of the cross as a sacrifice for our reconciliation. He shed his blood for our ransom and purification, so that we might be redeemed from our wretched state of bondage and cleansed from all sin. But to ensure that the memory of so great a gift would abide with us for ever, he left his body as food and his blood as drink for the faithful to consume in the form of bread and wine.

O precious and wonderful banquet, that brings us salvation and contains all sweetness! Could anything be of more intrinsic value? Under the old law it was the flesh of calves and goats that was offered, but here Christ himself, the true God, is set before us as our food. What could be more wonderful than this? No other sacrament has greater healing power; through it sins are purged away, virtues are increased, and the soul is enriched with an abundance of every spiritual gift. It is offered in the Church for the living and the dead, so that what was instituted for the salvation of all may be for the benefit of all. Yet, in the end, no one can fully express the sweetness of this sacrament, in which spiritual delight is tasted at its very source, and in which we renew the memory of that surpassing love for us which Christ revealed in his passion.

It was to impress the vastness of this love more firmly upon the hearts of the faithful that our Lord instituted this sacrament at the Last Supper. As he was on the point of leaving the world to go to the Father, after celebrating the Passover with his disciples, he left it as a perpetual memorial of his passion. It was the fulfillment of ancient figures and the greatest of all his miracles, while for those who were to experience the sorrow of his departure, it was destined to be a unique and abiding consolation.

Prayer

LORD Jesus Christ,
we worship you living among us
in the sacrament of your body and blood.

Be for us in this eucharist
strength to live the mystery of your presence.
May we offer to our Father in heaven
a solemn pledge of undivided love.
May we offer to our brothers and sisters
a life poured out in loving service of that kingdom
where you live with the Father and the Holy Spirit,
one God, for ever and ever.

(Opening Prayer, Corpus Christi)

*"You were slain and
have redeemed us
for our God in your blood."*

Crucifixion and death of Jesus

Luke 23:1-49

Jesus before Pilate

THE entire assembly rose up and led [Jesus] before Pilate. They started his prosecution by saying, "We found this man subverting our nation, opposing the payment of taxes to Caesar, and calling himself the Messiah, a king." Pilate asked him, "Are you the king of the Jews?" He answered, "That is your term." Pilate reported to the chief priests and the crowds, "I do not find a case against this man." But they insisted, "He stirs up the people by his teaching throughout the whole of Judea, from Galilee, where he began, to this very place." On hearing this Pilate asked if the man was a Galilean; and when he learned that he was under Herod's jurisdiction, he sent him to Herod, who also happened to be in Jerusalem at the time.

Herod was extremely please to see Jesus. From the reports about him he had wanted for a long time to see him, and he was hoping to see him work some miracle. He questioned Jesus at considerable length, but Jesus made no answer. The chief priests and scribes were at hand to accuse him vehemently. Herod and his guards then treated him with contempt and insult, after which they put a magnificent robe on him and sent him back to Pilate. Herod and Pilate, who had previously been set against each other, became friends from that day.

Jesus again before Pilate

Pilate then called together the chief priests, the ruling class, and the people, and said to them: "You have brought this man before me as one who subverts the people. I have examined him in your presence and have no charge against him arising from your allegations. Neither has Herod, who therefore has sent him back to us; obviously this man has done nothing that calls for death. Therefore I mean to release him, once I have taught him a lesson." The whole crowd cried out, "Away with this man; release Barabbas for us!" This Barabbas had been thrown in prison for causing an uprising in the city, and for murder. Pilate addressed them again, for he wanted Jesus to be the one he released.

But they shouted back. "Crucify him, crucify him!" He said to them for the third time, "What wrong is this man guilty of? I have not discovered anything about him that calls for the death penalty. I will therefore chastise him and release him." But they demanded with loud cries that he be crucified, and their shouts increased in violence. Pilate then decreed that what they demanded should be done. He released the one they asked for, who had been thrown in prison for insurrection and murder, and delivered Jesus up to their wishes.

The way of the cross

As they led him away, they laid hold of one Simon the Cyrenean who was coming in from the fields. They put a crossbeam on Simon's shoulder for him to carry along behind Jesus. A great crowd of people followed him, including women who beat their breasts and lamented over him. Jesus turned to them and said: "Daughters of Jerusalem, do not weep for me. Weep for yourselves and for your children. The days are coming when they will say, 'Happy are the sterile, the wombs that never bore and the breasts that never nursed.' Then they will begin saying to the mountains, 'Fall on us,' and to the hills, 'Cover us.' If they do these things in the green wood, what will happen in the dry?"

The Crucifixion

Two others who were criminals were led along with him to be crucified. When they came to Skull Place, as it was called, they crucified him there and the criminals as well, one on his right and the other on his left.

[Jesus said, "Father, forgive them; they do not know what they are doing."] They divided his garments, rolling dice for them.

The people stood watching, and the leaders kept jeering at him, saying, "He saved others; let him save himself if he is the Messiah of God, the chosen one." The soldiers also made fun of him, coming forward to offer him their sour wine and saying, "If you are the king of the Jews, save yourself." There was an inscription over his head:

"THIS IS THE KING OF THE JEWS."

One of the criminals hanging in crucifixion blasphemed him: "Aren't you the Messiah? Then save yourself and us." But the other one rebuked him: "Have you no fear of God, seeing you are under the same sentence? We deserve it, after all. We are only paying the price for what we've done, but this man has done nothing wrong." He then said, "Jesus, remember me when you enter upon your reign." And Jesus replied, "I assure you: this day you will be with me in paradise."

Jesus dies on the cross

It was now around midday, and darkness came over the whole land until midafternoon with an eclipse of the sun. The curtain in the sanctuary was torn in two. Jesus uttered a loud cry and said,

"Father, into your hands I commend my spirit."

After he said this, he expired. The centurion, upon seeing what had happened, gave glory to God by saying, "Surely this was an innocent man." When the crowd which had assembled for this spectacle saw what had happened, they went home beating their breasts. All his friends and the women who had accompanied him from Galilee were standing at a distance watching everything.

The lamb that was slain has delivered us from death and given us life

Melito of Sardis: *Easter homily*

THERE was much proclaimed by the prophets about the mystery of the Passover: that mystery is Christ, and to him be glory for ever and ever. Amen.

For the sake of suffering humanity he came down from heaven to earth, clothed himself in that humanity in the Virgin's womb, and was born a man. Having then a body capable of suffering, he took the pain of fallen man upon himself; he triumphed over the diseases of soul and body that were its cause, and by his Spirit, which was incapable of dying, he dealt man's destroyer, death, a fatal blow.

He was led forth like a lamb; he was slaughtered like a sheep. He ransomed us from our servitude to the world, as he had ransomed Israel from the land of Egypt; he freed us from our slavery to the devil, as he had freed Israel from the hand of Pharaoh. He sealed our souls with his own Spirit, and the members of our body with his own blood.

He is the One who covered death with shame and cast the devil into mourning, as Moses cast Pharaoh into mourning. He is the One who smote sin and robbed iniquity of offspring, as Moses robbed the Egyptians of their offspring. He is the One who brought us out of slavery into freedom, out of darkness into light, out of death into life, out of tyranny into an eternal kingdom; who made us a new priesthood, a people chosen to be his own for ever. He is the Passover that is our salvation.

It is he who endured every kind of suffering in all those who foreshadowed him. In Abel he was slain, in Isaac bound, in Jacob exiled, in Joseph sold, in Moses exposed to die. He was sacrificed in the Passover lamb, persecuted in David, dishonored in the prophets.

It is he who was made man of the Virgin, he who was hung on the tree; it is he who was buried in the earth, raised from the dead, and taken up to the heights of heaven. He is the mute lamb, the slain lamb, the lamb born of Mary, the fair ewe. He was seized from the flock, dragged off to be slaughtered, sacrificed in the evening, and buried at night. On the tree no bone of his was broken; in the earth his body knew no decay. He is the One who rose from the dead, and who raised man from the depths of the tomb.

Prayer

FATHER,
　　look with love upon your people,
the love which our Lord Jesus showed us
when he delivered himself to evil men
and suffered the agony of the cross,
for he lives and reigns with you and the Holy
　　Spirit,
one God, for ever and ever.

(Opening Prayer, Good Friday)

The burial of Jesus

Luke 23:50-56

THERE was a man named Joseph, an upright and holy member of the Sanhedrin, who had not been associated with their plan or their action. He was from Arimathea, a Jewish town, and he looked expectantly for the reign of God. This man approached Pilate with a request for Jesus' body. He took it down, wrapped it in fine linen, and laid it in a tomb hewn out of the rock, in which no one had yet been buried.

That was the Day of Preparation, and the sabbath was about to begin. The women who had come with him from Galilee followed along behind. They saw the tomb and how his body was buried. Then they went home to prepare spices and perfumes. They observed the sabbath as a day of rest, in accordance with the law.

The Lord descends into hell

Ancient homily

SOMETHING strange is happening—there is a great silence on earth today, a great silence and stillness. The whole earth keeps silence because the King is asleep. The earth trembled and is still because God has fallen asleep in the flesh and he has raised up all who have slept ever since the world began. God has died in the flesh and hell trembles with fear.

He has gone to search for our first parent, as for a lost sheep. Greatly desiring to visit those who live in darkness and in the shadow of death, he has gone to free from sorrow the captives Adam and Eve, he who is both God and the son of Eve. The Lord approached them bearing the cross, the weapon that had won him the victory. At the sight of him Adam, the first man he had created, struck his breast in terror and cried out to everyone: "My Lord be with you all." Christ answered him: "And with your spirit." He took him by the hand and raised him up, saying: "Awake, O sleeper, and rise from the dead, and Christ will give you light."

I am your God, who for your sake have become your son. Out of love for you and for your descendants I now by my own authority command all who are held in bondage to come forth, all who are in darkness to be enlightened, all who are sleeping to arise. I order you, O sleeper, to awake. I did not create you to be held a prisoner in hell. Rise from the dead, for I am the life of the dead. Rise up, work of my hands, you who were created in my image. Rise, let us leave this place, for you are in me and I am in you; together we form only one person and we cannot be separated.

For your sake I, your God, became your son; I, the Lord, took the form of a slave; I, whose home is above the heavens, descended to the earth and beneath the earth. For your sake, for the sake of man, I became like a man without help, free among the dead. For the sake of you, who left a garden, I am betrayed to the Jews in a garden, and I was crucified in a garden.

See on my face the spittle I received in order to restore to you the life I once breathed into you. See there the marks of the blows I received in order to refashion your warped nature in my image. On my back see the marks of the scourging I endured to remove the burden of sin that weighs upon your back. See my hands, nailed firmly to a tree, for you who once wickedly stretched out your hand to a tree.

I slept on the cross and a sword pierced my side for you who slept in paradise and brought forth Eve from your side. My side has healed the pain in yours. My sleep will rouse you from your sleep in hell. The sword that pierced me has sheathed the sword that was turned against you.

Rise, let us leave this place. The enemy led you out of the earthly paradise. I will not restore you to that paradise, but I will enthrone you in heaven. I forbade you the tree that was only a symbol of life, but see, I who am life itself am now one with you. I appointed cherubim to guard you as slaves are guarded, but now I make them worship you as God. The throne formed by cherubim awaits you, its bearers swift and eager. The bridal chamber is adorned, the banquet is ready, the eternal dwelling places are prepared, the treasure houses of all good things lie open. The kingdom of heaven has been prepared for you from all eternity.

Prayer

ALL-POWERFUL and ever-living God,
  your only Son went down among the dead
and rose again in glory.
In your goodness
raise up your faithful people,
buried with him in baptism,
to be one with him
in the eternal life of heaven,
where he lives and reigns with you and the Holy
   Spirit,
one God, for ever and ever.

(Prayer, Holy Saturday)

EASTER

The women at the tomb

Luke 24:1-12

ON THE first day of the week, at dawn, the women came to the tomb bringing the spices they had prepared. They found the stone rolled back from the tomb; but when they entered the tomb, they did not find the body of the Lord Jesus. While they were still at a loss over what to think of this, two men in dazzling garments stood beside them. Terrified, the women bowed to the ground. The men said to them: "Why do you search for the Living One among the dead? He is not here; he has been raised up. Remember what he said to you while he was still in Galilee —that the Son of Man must be delivered into the hands of sinful men, and be crucified, and on the third day rise again." With this reminder, his words came back to them.

On their return from the tomb, they told all these things to the Eleven and the others. The women were Mary of Magdala, Joanna, and Mary the mother of James. The other women with them also told the apostles, but the story seemed like nonsense and they refused to believe them. Peter, however, got up and ran to the tomb. He stooped down but could see nothing but the wrappings. So he went away full of amazement at what had occurred.

The cross of Christ gives life
to the human race

Ephrem: *Sermon*

DEATH trampled our Lord underfoot, but he in his turn treated death as a highroad for his own feet. He submitted to it, enduring it willingly, because by this means he would be able to destroy death in spite of itself. Death had its own way when our Lord went out from Jerusalem carrying his cross; but when by a loud cry from that cross he summoned the dead from the underworld, death was powerless to prevent it.

Death slew him by means of the body which he had assumed, but that same body proved to be the weapon with which he conquered death. Concealed beneath the cloak of his manhood, his godhead engaged death in combat; but in slaying our Lord, death itself was slain. It was able to kill natural human life, but was itself killed by the life that is above the nature of man.

Death could not devour our Lord unless he possessed a body, neither could hell swallow him up unless he bore our flesh; and so he came in search of a chariot in which to ride to the underworld. This chariot was the body which he received from the Virgin; in it he invaded death's fortress, broke open its strongroom and scattered all its treasure.

At length he came upon Eve, the mother of all the living. She was that vineyard whose enclosure her own hands had enabled death to violate, so that she could taste its fruit; thus the mother of all the living became the source of death for every living creature. But in her stead Mary grew up, a new vine in place of the old. Christ, the new life, dwelt within her. When death, with its customary imprudence, came foraging for her mortal fruit, it encountered its own destruction in the hidden life that fruit contained. All unsuspecting, it swallowed him up, and in so doing released life itself and set free a multitude of men.

He who was also the carpenter's glorious son set up his cross above death's all-consuming jaws, and led the human race into the dwelling place of life. Since a tree had brought about the downfall of mankind, it was upon a tree that mankind crossed over to the realm of life. Bitter was the branch that had once been grafted upon that ancient tree, but sweet the young shoot that has now been grafted in, the shoot in which we are meant to recognize the Lord whom no creature can resist.

We give glory to you, Lord, who raised up your cross to span the jaws of death like a bridge by which souls might pass from the region of the dead to the land of the living. We give glory to you who put on the body of a single mortal man and made it the source of life for every other mortal man. You are incontestably alive. Your murderers sowed your living body in the earth as farmers sow grain, but it sprang up and yielded an abundant harvest of men raised from the dead.

Come then, my brothers and sisters, let us offer our Lord the great and all-embracing sacrifice of our love, pouring out our treasury of hymns and prayers before him who offered his cross in sacrifice to God for the enrichment of us all.

Prayer

GOD our Father, creator of all,
today is the day of Easter joy.
This is the morning on which the Lord appeared
   to men
who had begun to lose hope
and opened their eyes to what the scriptures foretold:
that first he must die, and then he would rise
and ascend into his Father's glorious presence.

May the risen Lord
breathe on our minds and open our eyes
that we may know him in the breaking of bread,
and follow him in his risen life.
Grant this through Christ our Lord.

(Opening Prayer, Easter Sunday)

Jesus' final instruction and ascension

Acts 1:1-11

IN MY first account, Theophilus, I dealt with all that Jesus did and taught until the day he was taken up to heaven, having first instructed the apostles he had chosen through the Holy Spirit. In the time after his suffering he showed them in many convincing ways that he was alive, appearing to them over the course of forty days and speaking to them about the reign of God. On one occasion when he met with them, he told them not to leave Jerusalem: "Wait, rather, for the fulfillment of my Father's promise, of which you have heard me speak. John baptized with water, but within a few days you will be baptized with the Holy Spirit."

While they were with him they asked, "Lord, are you going to restore the rule to Israel now?" His answer was: "The exact time it is not yours to know. The Father has reserved that to himself. You will receive power when the Holy Spirit comes down on you; then you are to be my witnesses in Jerusalem, throughout Judea and Samaria, yes, even to the ends of the earth." No sooner had he said this than he was lifted up before their eyes in a cloud which took him from their sight.

They were still gazing up into the heavens when two men dressed in white stood beside them. "Men of Galilee," they said, "why do you stand here looking up at the skies? This Jesus who has been taken from you will return, just as you saw him go up into the heavens."

No one has ever ascended into heaven except the one who descended from heaven

Augustine: Sermon

TODAY our Lord Jesus Christ ascended into heaven; let our hearts ascend with him. Listen to the words of the Apostle: *If you have risen with Christ, set your hearts on the things that are above where Christ is, seated at the right hand of God; seek the things that are above, not the things that are on earth.* For just as he remained with us even after his ascension, so we too are already in heaven with him, even though what is promised us has not yet been fulfilled in our bodies.

Christ is now exalted above the heavens, but he still suffers on earth all the pain that we, the members of his body, have to bear. He showed this when he cried out from above: *Saul, Saul, why do you persecute me?* and when he said: *I was hungry and you gave me food.*

Why do we on earth not strive to find rest with him in heaven even now, through the faith, hope and love that unites us to him? While in heaven he is also with us; and we while on earth are with him. He is here with us by his divinity, his power and his love. We cannot be in heaven, as he is on earth, by divinity, but in him, we can be there by love.

He did not leave heaven when he came down to us; nor did he withdraw from us when he went up again into heaven. The fact that he was in heaven even while he was on earth is borne out by his own statement: *No one has ever ascended into heaven except the one who descended from heaven, the Son of Man, who is in heaven.*

Prayer

FATHER in heaven,
    our minds were prepared for the coming of
    your kingdom
when you took Christ beyond our sight
so that we might seek him in his glory.

May we follow where he has led
and find our hope in his glory,
for he is Lord for ever.

(Opening Prayer, Ascension)

PENTECOST

Jesus' appearance to the disciples

John 20:19-23

ON THE evening of that first day of the week, even though the disciples had locked the doors of the place where they were for fear of the Jews, Jesus came and stood before them. "Peace be with you," he said. When he had said this, he showed them his hands and his side. At the sight of the Lord the disciples rejoiced. "Peace be with you," he said again.

"As the Father has sent me,
so I send you."

Then he breathed on them and said:

"Receive the Holy Spirit.
If you forgive men's sins,
they are forgiven them;
if you hold them bound,
they are held bound."

The sending of the Holy Spirit

Irenaeus: *Against Heresies*

WHEN the Lord told his disciples *to go and teach all nations* and to *baptize them in the name of the Father and of the Son and of the*

Holy Spirit, he conferred on them the power of giving men new life in God.

He had promised through the prophets that in these last days he would pour out his Spirit on his servants and handmaids, and that they would prophesy. So when the Son of God became the Son of Man, the Spirit also descended upon him, becoming accustomed in this way to dwelling with the human race, to living in men and to inhabiting God's creation. The Spirit accomplished the Father's will in men who had grown old in sin, and gave them new life in Christ.

Luke says that the Spirit came down on the disciples at Pentecost, after the Lord's ascension, with power to open the gates of life to all nations and to make known to them the new covenant. So it was that men of every language joined in singing one song of praise to God, and scattered tribes, restored to unity by the Spirit, were offered to the Father as the firstfruits of all the nations.

This was why the Lord had promised to send the Advocate: he was to prepare us as an offering to God. Like dry flour, which cannot become one lump of dough, one loaf of bread, without moisture, we who are many could not become one in Christ Jesus without the water that comes down from heaven. And like parched ground, which yields no harvest unless it receives moisture, we who were once like a waterless tree could never have lived and borne fruit without this abundant rainfall from above. Through the baptism that liberates us from change and decay we have become one in body; through the Spirit we have become one in soul.

The Spirit of wisdom and understanding, the Spirit of counsel and strength, the Spirit of knowledge and the fear of God came down upon the Lord, and the Lord in turn gave this Spirit to his Church, sending the Advocate from heaven into all the world into which, according to his own words, the devil too had been cast down like lightning.

If we are not to be scorched and made unfruitful, we need the dew of God. Since we have our accuser, we need an Advocate as well. And so the Lord in his pity for man, who had fallen into the hands of brigands, having himself bound up his wounds and left for his care two coins bearing the royal image, entrusted him to the Holy Spirit. Now, through the Spirit, the image and inscription of the Father and the Son have been given to us, and it is our duty to use the coin committed to our charge and make it yield a rich profit for the Lord.

Prayer

FATHER of light, from whom every good gift comes,
send your Spirit into our lives
with the power of a mighty wind,
and by the flame of your wisdom
open the horizons of our minds.
Loosen our tongues to sing your praise
in words beyond the power of speech,
for without your Spirit
man could never raise his voice in words of peace

or announce the truth that Jesus is Lord,
who lives and reigns with you and the Holy
  Spirit,
one God, for ever and ever.

(Opening Prayer, Pentecost)

HOLY TRINITY

Commission of the apostles

Matthew 28:16-20

THE eleven disciples made their way to Galilee,
to the mountain to which Jesus had summoned them. At the sight of him, those who had
entertained doubts fell down in homage. Jesus
came forward and addressed them in these
words:

"Full authority has been given to me
both in heaven and on earth;
go, therefore, and make disciples of all the
  nations.
Baptize them in the name
  'of the Father,
  and of the Son,
  and of the Holy Spirit.'
Teach them to carry out everything I have
  commanded you.

And know that I am with you always, until the end of the world!"

I tasted and I saw

Catherine of Siena: *Dialogue*

ETERNAL God, eternal Trinity, you have made the blood of Christ so precious through his sharing in your divine nature. You are a mystery as deep as the sea; the more I search, the more I find, and the more I find, the more I search for you. But I can never be satisfied; what I receive will ever leave me desiring more. When you fill my soul I have an even greater hunger, and I grow more famished for your light. I desire above all to see you, the true light, as you really are.

I have tasted and seen the depth of your mystery and the beauty of your creation with the light of my understanding. I have clothed myself with your likeness and have seen what I shall be. Eternal Father, you have given me a share in your power and the wisdom that Christ claims as his own, and your Holy Spirit has given me the desire to love you. You are my Creator, eternal Trinity, and I am your creature. You have made of me a new creation in the blood of your Son, and I know that you are moved with love at the beauty of your creation, for you have enlightened me.

Eternal Trinity, Godhead, mystery deep as the sea, you could give me no greater gift than the gift of yourself. For you are a fire ever burning and never consumed, which itself consumes all the selfish love that fills my being. Yes, you are a fire that takes away the coldness, illuminates the mind with its light and causes me to know your truth. By this light, reflected as it were in a mirror, I recognize that you are the highest good, one we can neither comprehend nor fathom. And I know that you are beauty and wisdom itself. The food of angels, you gave yourself to man in the fire of your love.

You are the garment which covers our nakedness, and in our hunger you are a satisfying food, for you are sweetness and in you there is no taste of bitterness, O triune God!

Prayer

GOD, we praise you:
Father all-powerful, Christ Lord and Savior,
Spirit of love.
You reveal yourself in the depths of our being,
drawing us to share in your life and your love.
One God, three Persons,
be near to the people formed in your image,
close to the world your love brings to life.

We ask you this, Father, Son and Holy Spirit,
one God, true and living, for ever and ever.

(Opening Prayer, Trinity Sunday)

"O Mary, . . . you are the glory of Jerusalem,
the joy of Israel, the honor of our people."

READINGS AND PRAYERS
IN HONOR OF MARY,
THE MOTHER OF GOD

In praise of Mary,
Mother of God

Cyril of Alexandria: *Homily*

MARY, Mother of God, we salute you. Precious vessel worthy of the whole world's reverence, you are an ever-shining light, the crown of virginity, the symbol of orthodoxy, an indestructible temple, the place that held him whom no place can contain, mother and virgin. Because of you the holy gospels could say: *Blessed is he who comes in the name of the Lord.*

We salute you, for in your holy womb was confined him who is beyond all limitation. Because of you the holy Trinity is glorified and adored; the cross is called precious and is venerated throughout the world; the heavens exult; the angels and archangels make merry; demons are put to flight; the devil, that tempter, is thrust down from heaven; the fallen race of man is taken up on high; all creatures possessed by the madness of idolatry have attained knowledge of the truth; believers receive holy baptism; the oil of gladness is poured out; the Church is established throughout the world, pagans are brought to repentance.

What more is there to say? Because of you the light of the only-begotten Son of God has shone upon those who sat in darkness and in the shadow of death; prophets pronounced the word of God; the apostles preached salvation to the Gentiles; the dead are raised to life, and kings rule by the power of the holy Trinity.

Who can put Mary's high honor into words? She is both mother and virgin. I am overwhelmed by the wonder of this miracle.

The Hail Mary

HAIL Mary, full of grace,
the Lord is with you!
Blessed are you among women,
and blessed is the fruit of your womb, Jesus.
Holy Mary, Mother of God,
pray for us sinners,
now and at the hour of our death.

Hail holy Queen, Mother of mercy

HAIL, holy Queen, mother of mercy,
our life, our sweetness, and our hope.
To you do we cry,
poor banished children of Eve.
To you do we send up our sighs
mourning and weeping in this vale of tears.
Turn then, most gracious advocate,
your eyes of mercy toward us,
and after this exile

show us the blessed fruit of your womb,
  Jesus.
O clement, O loving,
O sweet Virgin Mary.

Remember, O most gracious Virgin Mary

REMEMBER, O most gracious Virgin Mary,
  that never was it known that anyone who
    fled to your protection,
implored your help, or sought your intercession
  was left unaided.
Inspired by this confidence, we fly unto you,
O Virgin of virgins, our Mother!
To you we come, before you we stand, sinful
  and sorrowful.
O Mother of the Word incarnate,
despise not our petitions,
but in your mercy hear and answer us.
Amen.

You are all fair, O Mary

YOU are all fair, O Mary,
  And the original stain is not in you.
You are the glory of Jerusalem,
The joy of Israel,
The honor of our people,
The advocate of sinners.
O Mary,
Virgin most prudent,
Mother most merciful,
Pray for us,
Intercede for us with our Lord Jesus Christ.

Loving Mother of the Redeemer

LOVING mother of the Redeemer,
    gate of heaven, star of the sea,
assist your people who have fallen yet strive to
    rise again.
To the wonderment of nature you bore your
    Creator,
yet remained a virgin after as before.
You received Gabriel's joyful greeting,
have pity on us poor sinners.

Mary proclaims the greatness
of the Lord working in her

Bede the Venerable: *Homily*

MY SOUL *proclaims the greatness of the
Lord, and my spirit rejoices in God my
savior.* With these words Mary first acknowl-
edges the special gifts she has been given. Then
she recalls God's universal favors, bestowed
unceasingly on the human race.

When a man devotes all his thoughts to the
praise and service of the Lord, he proclaims
God's greatness. His observance of God's commands, moreover, shows that he has God's
power and greatness always at heart. His spirit
rejoices in God his savior and delights in the
mere recollection of his creator who gives him
hope for eternal salvation.

These words are often for all God's crea-
tions, but especially for the Mother of God.
She alone was chosen, and she burned with
spiritual love for the son she so joyously conceived. Above all other saints, she alone could

truly rejoice in Jesus, her savior, for she knew
that he who was the source of eternal salvation would be born in time in her body, in one
person both her own son and her Lord.

*For the Almighty has done great things for
me, and holy is his name.* Mary attributes
nothing to her own merits. She refers all her
greatness to the gift of the one whose essence
is power and whose nature is greatness, for he
fills with greatness and strength the small and
the weak who believe in him.

She did well to add: *and holy is his name*, to
warn those who heard, and indeed all who
would receive his words, that they must believe and call upon his name. For they too
could share in everlasting holiness and true
salvation according to the words of the prophet: *and it will come to pass, that everyone who
calls on the name of the Lord will be saved.*
This is the name she spoke of earlier: *and my
spirit rejoices in God my savior.*

Therefore it is an excellent and fruitful custom of holy Church that we should sing Mary's
hymn at the time of evening prayer. By meditating upon the incarnation, our devotion is
kindled, and by remembering the example of
God's Mother, we are encouraged to lead a life
of virtue. Such virtues are best achieved in the
evening. We are weary after the day's work
and worn out by our distractions. The time for
rest is near, and our minds are ready for contemplation.

THE ROSARY

THE rosary is a devotional prayer that has been treasured in the church for centuries. Its succession of Hail Marys recalls the Incarnation of Jesus Christ, when Mary accepted the invitation of the angel and became the Mother of God. With her whole being she received God's Son and became his companion in the mysteries of his life. Praying the rosary we accept the Lord's invitation to be with us and join the Holy Virgin devotedly sharing his life.

The rosary is a summary of Christian faith, recalling the principal mysteries accomplished in Christ, from his birth and childhood, to his Passion and Resurrection, and finally to his blessing of the infant church at Pentecost and of Mary crowned Queen of Heaven. Christ who emptied himself and was born in the likeness of men, who humbled himself obediently accepting even death on a cross, who was exalted and glorified, is praised in the mysteries of the rosary.

In the rosary we approach Jesus with Mary who "kept all these things in mind, treasuring them in her heart." This prayer should be recited sharing Mary's own prayerful spirit. "By its nature the recitation of the rosary calls for a quiet rhythm and a lingering pace, helping the individual to meditate on the mysteries of the Lord's life as seen through the eyes of her who was closest to the Lord. In this way the unfathomable riches of these mysteries are unfolded" (Pope Paul VI).

The mysteries of the rosary can be announced before the Our Father and the decade of Hail Marys.

Another custom for meditating on the mysteries, especially suited for those who recite the rosary often and alone, is to add to the name of Jesus in each Hail Mary a reference to the mystery being recalled.

For example, when you meditate on the joyful mysteries, say the Hail Mary in this way:

Hail Mary, full of grace . . . and blessed is the fruit of your womb, Jesus

(1) whom you conceived at the message of an angel.
(2) whom you carried within you on your visit to Elizabeth.
(3) who was born to you at Bethlehem.
(4) whom you presented in the Temple.
(5) whom you found in the Temple.

The sorrowful mysteries:
(1) who agonized for us in the garden.
(2) who was scourged for us.
(3) who was crowned with thorns for us.
(4) who carried his cross for us.
(5) who was crucified for us.

The glorious mysteries:
(1) who rose from the dead.
(2) who ascended into heaven.
(3) who sent the Holy Spirit.
(4) who took you up into heaven.
(5) who crowned you Queen of Heaven.

"We seek from the saints example in their way of life, fellowship in their communion, and aid by their intercession" (Vatican II).

READINGS AND PRAYERS
FROM THE SAINTS
AND SPIRITUAL WRITERS

The song of the Church

Pius X: *Apostolic Constitution*

THE collection of psalms found in Scripture, composed as it was under divine inspiration, has, from the very beginnings of the Church, shown a wonderful power of fostering devotion among Christians as they offer to *God a continuous sacrifice of praise, the harvest of lips blessing his name.* Following a custom already established in the Old Law, the psalms have played a conspicuous part in the sacred liturgy itself, and in the divine office.

The psalms have also a wonderful power to awake in our hearts the desire for every virtue. Athanasius says: *Though all Scripture, both old and new, is divinely inspired and has its use in teaching, as we read in Scripture itself yet the Book of Psalms, like a garden enclosing the fruits of all the other books, produces their fruits in song, and in the process of singing brings forth its own special fruits to take their place beside them.* In the same place Athanasius rightly adds: *The psalms seem to me to be like a mirror, in which the person using them can see himself, and the stirrings of his own heart; he can recite them against the background of his own emotions.* Augustine says in his Confessions: *How I wept when I heard your hymns and canticles, being deeply moved by the sweet singing of your Church. Those voices flowed into my ears, truth filtered into my heart, and from my heart surged waves of devotion. Tears ran down, and I was happy in my tears.*

Indeed, who could fail to be moved by those many passages in the psalms which set forth so profoundly the infinite majesty of God, his omnipotence, his justice and goodness and clemency, too deep for words, and all the other infinite qualities of his that deserve our praise? Who could fail to be roused to the same emotions by the prayers of thanksgiving to God for blessings received, by the petitions, so humble and confident, for blessings still awaited, by the cries of a soul in sorrow for sin committed? Who would not be fired with love as he looks on the likeness of Christ, the redeemer, here so lovingly foretold? His was *the voice* Augustine *heard in every psalm, the voice of praise, of suffering, of joyful expectation, of present distress.*

The glorious duty of man: to pray and to love

John Mary Vianney, *Catechetical instructions*

MY LITTLE children, reflect on these words: the Christian's treasure is not on earth but in heaven. Our thoughts, then, ought to be directed to where our treasure is. This is the glorious duty of man: to pray and to love. If you pray and love, that is where a man's happiness lies.

Prayer is nothing else but union with God. When one has a heart that is pure and united with God, he is given a kind of serenity and sweetness that makes him ecstatic, a light that surrounds him with marvelous brightness. In this intimate union, God and the soul are fused together like two bits of wax that no one can ever pull apart. This union of God with a tiny creature is a lovely thing. It is a happiness beyond understanding.

We had become unworthy to pray, but God in his goodness allowed us to speak with him. Our prayer is incense that gives him the greatest pleasure.

My little children, your hearts are small, but prayer stretches them and makes them capable of loving God. Through prayer we receive a foretaste of heaven and something of paradise comes down upon us. Prayer never leaves us without sweetness. It is honey that flows into the soul and makes all things sweet. When we pray properly, sorrows disappear like snow before the sun.

Your kingdom come

Teresa of Avila: *Way of Perfection*

WHEN asking a favor of some person of importance would anyone be so ill-mannered and thoughtless as not first to consider how best to address him in order to make a good impression and give him no cause for offense? Surely he would think over his petition carefully and his reason for making it, especially if it were for something specific and important as our good Jesus tells us our petitions should be. It seems to me that this point deserves serious attention. My Lord, could you not have included all in one word by saying: "Father, give us whatever is good for us"? After all, to one who understands everything so perfectly, what need is there to say more?

O Eternal Wisdom, between you and your Father that was enough; that was how you prayed in the garden. You expressed your desire and fear but surrendered yourself to his will. But as for us, my Lord, you know that we are less submissive to the will of your Father and need to mention each thing separately in order to stop and think whether it would be good for us, and otherwise not ask for it. You see, the gift our Lord intends for us may be by far the best, but if it is not what we wanted we are quite capable of flinging it back in his face. That is the kind of people we are; ready cash is the only wealth we understand.

Therefore, the good Jesus bids us repeat these words, this prayer for his kingdom to come in us: *Hallowed be your name, your kingdom come.* See how wise our Master is! But what do we mean when we pray for this kingdom? That is what I am going to consider now, for it is important that we should understand it. Our good Jesus placed these two petitions side by side because he realized that in our inadequacy we could never fittingly

hallow, praise, exalt or glorify this holy name of
the eternal Father unless he enabled us to do so
by giving us his kingdom here on earth. But since
we must know what we are asking for and how
important it is to pray for it without ceasing and
to do everything in our power to please him who
is to give it to us, I should now like to give you
my own thoughts on the matter.

Of the many joys that are found in the kingdom of heaven, the greatest seems to me to be
the sense of tranquility and well-being that we
shall experience when we are free from all concern for earthly things. Glad because others are
glad and for ever at peace, we shall have the deep
satisfaction of seeing that by all creatures the
Lord is honored and praised, and his name blessed. No one ever offends him, for there everyone
loves him. Loving him is the soul's one concern.
Indeed it cannot help but love him, for it knows
him. Here below our love must necessarily fall
short of that perfection and constancy, but even
so how different it would be, how much more
like that of heaven, if we really knew our Lord!

Our daily work is to do the will
of God

Elizabeth Seton: *Conference*

I WILL tell you what is my own great help. I
once read or heard that an interior life means
but the continuation of our Savior's life in us;
that the great object of all his mysteries is to
merit for us the grace of his interior life and
communicate it to us, it being the end of his mission to lead us into the sweet land of promise, a

life of constant union with himself. And what was the first rule of our dear Savior's life? You know it was to do his Father's will. Well, then, the first end I propose in our daily work is to do the will of God; secondly, to do it in the manner he wills; and thirdly, to do it because it is his will.

I know what his will is by those who direct me; whatever they bid me do, if it is ever so small in itself, is the will of God for me. Then do it in the manner he wills it, not sewing an old thing as if it were new, or a new thing as if it were old; not fretting because the oven is too hot, or in a fuss because it is too cold. You understand —not flying and driving because you are hurried, not creeping like a snail because no one pushes you. Our dear Savior was never in extremes. The third object is to do his will *because* God wills it, that is, to be ready to quit at any moment and to do anything else to which you may be called. . .

You think it very hard to lead a life of such restraint unless you keep your eye of faith always open. Perseverance is a great grace. To go on gaining and advancing every day, we must be resolute, and bear and suffer as our blessed forerunners did. Which of them gained heaven without a struggle? . . .

What are our real trials? By what name shall we call them? One cuts herself out a cross of pride; another, one of causeless discontent; another, one of restless impatience or peevish fretfulness. But is the whole any better than children's play if looked at with the common eye of faith? Yet we know certainly that our God calls us to a holy life, that he gives us every grace, every abundant grace; and though we are so weak of ourselves, this grace is able to carry us through every obstacle and difficulty.

But we lack courage to keep a continual watch over nature, and therefore, year after year, with our thousand graces, multiplied resolutions, and fair promises, we run around in a circle of misery and imperfections. After a long time in the service of God, we come nearly to the point from whence we set out, and perhaps with even less ardor for penance and mortification than when we began our consecration to him.

You are now in your first setout. Be above the vain fears of nature and efforts of your enemy. You are children of eternity. Your immortal crown awaits you, and the best of Fathers waits there to reward your duty and love. You may indeed sow here in tears, but you may be sure there to reap in joy.

Put Christ before everything

Benedict: *Rule*

WHENEVER you begin any good work you should first of all make a most pressing appeal to Christ our Lord to bring it to perfection; that he, who has honored us by counting us among his children, may never be grieved by our evil deeds. For we must always serve him with the good things he has given us in such a way that he may never—as an angry father disinherits his sons or even like a master who inspires fear—grow impatient with our sins and consign us to everlasting punishment, like wicked servants who would not follow him to glory.

So we should at long last rouse ourselves, prompted by the words of Scripture: *Now is the time for us to rise from sleep.* Our eyes should be open to the God-given light, and we should listen in wonderment to the message of the divine voice as it daily cries out: *Today, if you shall hear his voice, harden not your hearts;* and again: *If anyone has ears to hear, let him listen to what the Spirit is saying to the churches.* And what does the Spirit say? *Come my sons, listen to me; I will teach you the fear of the Lord. Hurry, while you have the light of life, so that death's darkness may not overtake you.*

On the love of Christ

Alphonsus Liguori: *Sermon*

ALL holiness and perfection of soul lies in our love for Jesus Christ our God, who is our redeemer and our supreme good. It is part of the love of God to acquire and to nurture all the virtues which make a man perfect.

Has not God in fact won for himself a claim on all our love? From all eternity he has loved us. And it is in this vein that he speaks to us: "O man, consider carefully that I first loved you. You had not yet appeared in the light of day, nor did the world yet exist, but already I loved you. From all eternity I have loved you."

Since God knew that man is enticed by favors, he wished to bind him to his love by means of his gifts: "I want to catch men with the snares, those chains of love in which they allow themselves to be entrapped, so that they will love me." And all the gifts which he bestowed on man were given to this end. He gave him a soul, made in his likeness, and endowed with memory, intellect and will; he gave him a body equipped with the senses; it was for him that he created heaven and earth and such an abundance of things. He made all these things out of love for man, so that all creation might serve man, and man in turn might love God out of gratitude for so many gifts.

But he did not wish to give us only beautiful creatures; the truth is that to win for himself our love, he went so far as to bestow upon us the **fullness of himself.** The eternal Father went so far as to give his Son. When he saw that we were all dead through sin and deprived of his grace, what did he do? Compelled, as the Apostle says, by the superabundance of his love for us, he sent his beloved Son to make reparation for us and to call us back to a sinless life.

By giving us his Son, whom he did not spare precisely so that he might spare us, he bestowed on us at once every good: grace, love and heaven; for all these goods are certainly inferior to the Son. *He who did not spare his own Son, but handed him over for all of us; how could he fail to give us along with his Son all good things?*

Serving the poor is to be our first preference

Vincent de Paul: *Letter*

EVEN though the poor are often rough and un-refined, we must not judge them from external appearances nor from the mental gifts they seem to have received. On the contrary, if you consider the poor in the light of faith, then you will observe that they are taking the place of the Son of God who chose to be poor. Although in his passion he almost lost the appearance of a man and was considered a fool by the Gentiles and a stumbling block by the Jews, he showed them that his mission was to preach to the poor: *He sent me to preach the good news to the poor.* We also ought to have this same spirit and imitate Christ's actions, that is, we must take care of the poor, console them, help them, support their cause.

We preach Christ crucified

Paul of the Cross: *Letter*

IT IS very good and holy to consider the passion of our Lord and to meditate on it, for by this sacred path we reach union with God. In this most holy school we learn true wisdom, for it was there that all the saints learned it. Indeed when the cross of our dear Jesus has planted its roots more deeply in your hearts, then will you rejoice: "To suffer and not to die," or, "Either to suffer or to die," or better: "Neither to suffer, nor to die, but only to turn perfectly to the will of God."

Love is a unifying virtue which takes upon itself the torments of its beloved Lord. It is a fire reaching through to the inmost soul. It transforms the lover into the one loved. More deeply, love intermingles with grief, and grief with love, and a certain blending of love and grief occurs. They become so united that we can no longer distinguish love from grief nor grief from love.

Thus the loving heart rejoices in its sorrow and exults in its grieving love.

Therefore, be constant in practicing every virtue, and especially in imitating the patience of our dear Jesus, for this is the summit of pure love. Live in such a way that all may know that you bear outwardly as well as inwardly the image of Christ crucified, the model of all gentleness and mercy. For if a man is united inwardly with the Son of the living God, he also bears his likeness outwardly by his continual practice of heroic goodness, and especially through a patience reinforced by courage, which does not complain either secretly or in public. Conceal yourselves in Jesus crucified, and hope for nothing except that all men be thoroughly converted to his will.

When you become true lovers of the Crucified, you will always celebrate the feast of the cross in the inner temple of the soul, bearing all in silence and not relying on any creature. Since festivals ought to be celebrated joyfully, those who love the Crucified should honor the feast of the cross by enduring in silence with a serene and joyful countenance, so that their suffering remains hidden from men and is observed by God alone. For in this feast there is always a solemn banquet, and the food presented is the will of God, exemplified by the love of our crucified Christ.

Wherein sin abounded
grace has overflowed

Bernard: *Sermon on the Songs of Songs*

WHERE can the weak find a place of firm security and peace, except in the wounds of the Savior? Indeed, the more secure is my place there the more he can do to help me. The world rages, the flesh is heavy, and the devil lays his snares, but I do not fall, for my feet are planted on firm rock. I may have sinned gravely. My conscience would be distressed, but it would not be in turmoil, for I would recall the wounds of the Lord: *he was wounded for our iniquities.* What sin is there so deadly that it cannot be pardoned by the death of Christ? And so if I bear in mind this strong, effective remedy, I can never again be terrified by the malignancy of sin.

Surely the man who said, *My sin is too great to merit pardon,* was wrong. He was speaking as though he were not a member of Christ and had no share in his merits, so that he could claim them as his own, as a member of the body can claim what belongs to the head. As for me, what can I appropriate that I lack from the heart of the Lord who abounds in mercy? They pierced his hands and feet and opened his side with a spear. Through the openings of these wounds I may drink *honey from the rock and oil from the hardest stone:* that is, I may *taste and see that the Lord is sweet.*

He was thinking thoughts of peace, and I did not know it, *for who knows the mind of the Lord, or who has been his counselor?* But the piercing nail has become a key to unlock the door, that I may see the good will of the Lord. And what can I see as I look through the hole? Both the nail and the wound cry out that God was in Christ reconciling the world to himself. *The sword pierced his soul and came close to his heart,* so that he might be able to feel compassion for me in my weaknesses.

Through these sacred wounds we can see the secret of his heart, the great mystery of love, *the sincerity of his mercy with which he visited us from on high.* Where have your love, your mercy, your compassion shone out more luminously than in your wounds, sweet, gentle Lord of mercy? More mercy than this no one has than that he lay down his life for those who are doomed to death.

The knowledge of the mystery hidden in Christ Jesus

John of the Cross: *Spiritual Canticle*

THOUGH holy doctors have uncovered many mysteries and wonders, and devout souls have understood them in this earthly condition of ours, yet the greater part still remains to be unfolded by them, and even to be understood by them.

We must then dig deeply in Christ. He is like a rich mine with many pockets containing treasures: however deep we dig we will never find their end or their limit. Indeed, in every pocket new seams of fresh riches are discovered on all sides.

For this reason the apostle Paul said of Christ: *In him are hidden all the treasures of the wisdom and knowledge of God.* The soul cannot enter into these treasures, nor attain them, unless it first crosses into and enters the thicket of suffering, enduring interior and exterior labors, and unless it first receives from God very many blessings in the intellect and in the senses, and has undergone long spiritual training.

All these are lesser things, disposing the soul for the lofty sanctuary of the knowledge of the mysteries of Christ: this is the highest wisdom attainable in this life.

Would that men might come at last to see that it is quite impossible to reach the thicket of the riches and wisdom of God except by first entering the thicket of much suffering, in such a way that the soul finds there its consolation and desire. The soul that longs for divine wisdom chooses first, and in truth, to enter the thicket of the cross.

Saint Paul therefore urges the Ephesians *not to grow weary in the midst of tribulations,* but to be *rooted and grounded in love, so that they may know with all the saints the breadth, the length, the height and the depth—to know what is beyond knowledge, the love of Christ, so as to be filled with all the fullness of God.*

The gate that gives entry into these riches of his wisdom is the cross; because it is a narrow gate, while many seek the joys that can be gained through it, it is given to few to desire to pass through it.

———

She longed for Christ,
though she thought he had been taken away

Gregory the Great: *Homily*

WHEN Mary Magdalene came to the tomb and did not find the Lord's body, she thought it had been taken away and so informed the disciples. After they came and saw the tomb, they too believed what Mary had told them. The text then says: *The disciples went back home,* and it adds: *but Mary wept and remained standing outside the tomb.*

We should reflect on Mary's attitude and the great love she felt for Christ; for though the disciples had left the tomb, she remained. She was still seeking the one she had not found, and while she sought she wept; burning with the fire of love, she longed for him who she thought had been taken away. And so it happened that the woman who stayed behind to seek Christ was the only one to see him. For perseverance is essential to any good deed, as the voice of truth tells us: *Whoever perseveres to the end will be saved.*

At first she sought but did not find, but when she persevered it happened that she found what she was looking for. When our desires are not satisfied, they grow stronger, and becoming stronger they take hold of their object. Holy desires likewise grow with anticipation, and if they do not grow they are not really desires. Anyone who succeeds in attaining the truth has burned with such a love. As David says: *My soul has thirsted for the living God; when shall I come and appear before the face of God?* And so also in the Song of Songs the Church says: *I was wounded by love;* and again: *My soul is melted with love.*

Woman, why are you weeping? Whom do you seek? She is asked why she is sorrowing so that her desire might be strengthened; for when she mentions whom she is seeking, her love is kindled all the more ardently.

Jesus says to her: Mary. Jesus is not recognized when he calles her "woman"; so he calls her by name, as though he were saying: Recognize me as I recognize you; for I do not know you as I know others; I know you as yourself. And so Mary, once addressed by name, recognizes who is speaking. She immediately calls him *rabboni,* that is to say, *teacher,* because the one whom she sought outwardly was the one who inwardly taught her to keep on searching.

All my hope lies in your great mercy

Augustine: *Confessions*

WHERE did I find you, that I came to know you? You were not within my memory before I learned of you. Where, then, did I find you before I came to know you, if not within yourself, far above me? We come to you and go from you, but no place is involved in this process. In every place, O Truth, you are present to those who seek your help, and at once and the same time you answer all, though they seek your counsel on different matters.

You respond clearly, but not everyone hears clearly. All ask what they wish, but do not always hear the answer they wish. Your best servant is he who is intent not so much on hearing his petition answered, as rather on willing whatever he hears from you.

Late have I loved you, O Beauty ever ancient, ever new, late have I loved you! You were within me, but I was outside, and it was there that I searched for you. In my unloveliness I plunged into the lovely things which you created. You were with me, but I was not with you. Created things kept me from you; yet if they had not been in you they would not have been at all. You called, you shouted, and you broke through my deafness. You flashed your fragrance on me; I drew in breath and now I pant for you. I have tasted you; now I hunger and thirst for more. You touched me, and I burned for your peace.

When once I shall be united to you with my whole being, I shall at last be free of sorrow and toil. Then my life will be alive, filled entirely with you. When you fill someone, you relieve him of his burden, but because I am not yet filled with you, I am a burden to myself. My joy when I should be weeping struggles with my sorrows when I should be rejoicing. I know not where victory lies. Woe is me! Lord, have mercy on me! My evil sorrows and good joys are at war with one another. I know not where victory lies. Woe is me! Lord, have mercy! Woe is me! I make no effort to conceal my wounds. You are my physician, I am your patient. You are merciful; I stand in need of mercy.

God's temple is holy;
you are his temple

Ambrose: *Exposition of Psalm* 118

MY FATHER *and I will come and make our home with him:* Let your door stand open to receive him, unlock your soul to him, offer him a welcome in your mind, and then you will see the riches of simplicity, the treasures of peace, the joy of grace. Throw wide the gate of your heart, stand before the sun of the ever-lasting light *that shines on every man.* This true light shines on all, but if anyone closes his window he will deprive himself of eternal light. If you shut the door of your mind, you shut out Christ. Though he can enter, he does not want to force his way in rudely, or compel us to admit him against our will.

Born of a virgin, he came forth from the womb as the light of the whole world in order to shine on all men. His light is received by those who long for the splendor of perpetual light that night can never destroy. The sun of our daily experience is succeeded by the dark-ness of night, but the sun of holiness never sets, because wisdom cannot give place to evil.

Blessed then is the man at whose door Christ stands and knocks. Our door is faith; if it is strong enough, the whole house is safe. This is the door by which Christ enters. So the Church says in the Song of Songs: *The voice of my brother is at the door.* Hear his knock, listen to him asking to enter: *Open to me, my sister, my betrothed, my dove, my perfect one, for my head*

*is covered with dew, and my hair with the mois-
ture of the night.*

When does God the Word most often knock
at your door? — When his head is covered with
the dew of night. He visits in love those in trouble and temptation to save them from being
overwhelmed by their trials. His head is covered with dew or moisture when those who are
his body are in distress. That is the time when
you must keep watch so that when the bridegroom comes he may not find himself shut out,
and take his departure. If you were to sleep, if
your heart were not wide awake, he would not
knock but go away; but if your heart is watchful, he knocks and asks you to open the door to
him.

Our soul has a door; it has gates. *Lift up your
heads, O gates, and be lifted up, eternal gates,
and the King of glory will enter.* If you open the
gates of your faith, the King of glory will enter
your house in the triumphal procession in honor
of his passion. Holiness too has its gates. We
read in Scripture what the Lord Jesus said
through his prophet: *Open for me the gates of
holiness.*

It is the soul that has its door, its gates. Christ
comes to this door and knocks; he knocks at
these gates. Open to him; he wants to enter; to
find his bride waiting and watching.

The living water of the Holy Spirit

Cyril of Jerusalem: *Catechetical Instruction*

THE water that I shall give him will become in him a fountain of living water, *welling up into eternal life.* This is a new kind of water, a living, leaping water, welling up for those who are worthy. But why did Christ call the grace of the Spirit water? Because all things are dependent on water; plants and animals have their origin in water. Water comes down from heaven as rain, and although it is always the same in itself, it produces many different effects, one in the palm tree, another in the vine, and so on throughout the whole of creation. It does not come down, now as one thing, now as another, but while remaining essentially the same, it adapts itself to the needs of every creature that receives it.

In the same way the Holy Spirit, whose nature is always the same, simple and indivisible, apportions grace to each man as he wills. Like a dry tree which puts forth shoots when watered, the soul bears the fruit of holiness when repentance has made it worthy of receiving the Holy Spirit. Although the Spirit never changes, the effects of his action, by the will of God and in the name of Christ, are both many and marvelous.

The Spirit makes one man a teacher of divine truth, inspires another to prophesy, gives another the power of casting out devils, enables another to interpret holy Scripture. The Spirit strengthens one man's self-control, shows another how to help the poor, teaches another to fast and lead a life of asceticism, makes another oblivious to the needs of the body, trains another for martyrdom. His action is different in different people, but the Spirit himself is always the same. *In each person,* Scripture says, *the Spirit reveals his presence in a particular way for the common good.*

The Spirit comes gently and makes himself known by his fragrance. He is not felt as a burden, for he is light, very light. Rays of light and knowledge stream before him as he approaches. The Spirit comes with the tenderness of a true friend and protector to save, to heal, to teach, to counsel, to strengthen, to console. The Spirit comes to enlighten the mind first of the one who receives him, and then, through him, the minds of others as well.

As light strikes the eyes of a man who comes out of darkness into the sunshine and enables him to see clearly things he could not discern before, so light floods the soul of the man counted worthy of receiving the Holy Spirit and enables him to see things beyond the range of human vision, things hitherto undreamed of.

Devotion must be practiced in different ways

Francis de Sales: *Introduction to the Devout Life*

WHEN God the Creator made all things, he commanded the plants to bring forth fruit each according to its own kind; he has likewise commanded Christians, who are the living plants of his Church, to bring forth the fruits of devotion, each one in accord with his character, his station and his calling.

I say that devotion must be practiced in different ways by the nobleman and by the working man, by the servant and by the prince, by the widow, by the unmarried girl and by the married woman. But even this distinction is not sufficient; for the practice of devotion must be adapted to the strength, to the occupation and to the duties of each one in particular.

Tell me, please, my Philothea, whether it is proper for a bishop to want to lead a solitary life like a Carthusian; or for married people to be no more concerned than a Capuchin about increasing their income; or for a working man to spend his whole day in church like a religious; or on the other hand for a religious to be constantly exposed like a bishop to all the events and circumstances that bear on the needs of our neighbor. Is not this sort of devotion ridiculous, unorganized and intolerable? Yet this absurd error occurs very frequently, but in no way does true devotion, my Philothea, destroy anything at all. On the contrary, it perfects and fulfills all things. In fact if it ever works against, or is inimical to, anyone's legitimate station and calling, then it is very definitely false devotion.

The bee collects honey from flowers in such a way as to do the least damage or destruction to them, and he leaves them whole, undamaged and fresh, just as he found them. True devotion does still better. Not only does it not injure any sort of calling or occupation, it even embellishes and enhances it.

Moreover, just as every sort of gem, cast in honey, becomes brighter and more sparkling,

each according to its color, so each person becomes more acceptable and fitting in his own vocation when he sets his vocation in the context of
devotion. Through devotion your family cares become more peaceful, mutual love between husband and wife becomes more sincere, the service
we owe to the prince becomes more faithful, and
our work, no matter what it is, becomes more
pleasant and agreeable.

In the heart of the Church
I will be love

Theresa of the Child Jesus: *Autobiography*

SINCE my longing for martyrdom was powerful and unsettling, I turned to the epistles of
Saint Paul in the hope of finally finding an answer. By chance the twelfth and thirteenth chap-
ters of the first epistle to the Corinthians caught
my attention, and in the first section I read that
not everyone can be an apostle, prophet or teacher, that the Church is composed of a variety of
members, and that the eye cannot be the hand.
Even with such an answer revealed before me, I
was not satisfied and did not find peace.

I persevered in the reading and did let not my
mind wander until I found this encouraging
theme: *Set your desires on the greater gifts. And
I will now show you the way which surpasses all
others.* For the Apostle insists that the greater
gifts are nothing at all without love and that this
same love is surely the best path leading directly
to God. At length I had found peace of mind.

When I had looked upon the mystical body of the Church, I recognized myself in none of the members which Saint Paul described, and what is more, I desired to distinguish myself more favorably within the whole body. Love appeared to me to be the hinge for my vocation. Indeed I knew that the Church had a body composed of various members, but in this body the necessary and more noble member was not lacking; I knew that the Church had a heart and that such a heart appeared to be aflame with love. I knew that one love drove the members of the Church to action, that if this love were extinguished, the apostles would have proclaimed the Gospel no longer, the martyrs would have shed their blood no more. I saw and realized that love sets off the bounds of all vocations, that love is everything, that this same love embraces every time and every place. In one word, that love is everlasting.

Then, nearly ecstatic with the supreme joy in my soul, I proclaimed: O Jesus, my love, at last I have found my calling: my call is love. Certainly I have found my proper place in the Church, and you gave me that very place, my God. In the heart of the Church, my mother, I will be love, and thus I will be all things, as my desire finds its direction.

Canticle of the Sun

Francis of Assisi

OH, MOST HIGH, Almighty, Good Lord God, to Thee belong praise, glory, honor and all blessing.

Praised be my Lord God, with all His creatures,
and especially our brother the Sun, who brings
us the day and who brings us the light: fair is
he, and he shines with a very great splendor.
O Lord, he signifies us to thee!

Praised be my Lord for our sister the Moon, and
for the stars, the which He has set clear and
lovely in the heaven.

Praised be my Lord for our brother the wind, and
for air and clouds, calms and all weather, by
which Thou upholdest life and all creatures.

Praised be my Lord for our sister water, who is
very serviceable to us, and humble and precious and clean.

Praised be my Lord for our brother fire, through
whom Thou givest us light in the darkness; and
he is bright and pleasant and very mighty and
strong.

Praised be my Lord for our mother the earth, the
which doth sustain us and keep us, and bring-
eth forth divers fruits and flowers of many
colors, and grass.

Praised be my Lord for all those who pardon one
another for love's sake, and who endure weakness and tribulation: blessed are they who
peacefully shall endure, for Thou, O Most
High, wilt give them a crown.

Praised be my Lord for our sister, the death of
the body, from which no man escapeth. Woe to
him who dieth in mortal sin. Blessed are those
who die in Thy most holy will, for the second
death shall have no power to do them harm.

Praise ye and bless the Lord, and give thanks to
Him and serve Him with great humility.

Prayer of St. Patrick

Translator: Kuno Meyer

I ARISE to-day
   Through a mighty strength, the invocation
  of the Trinity,
Through belief in the threeness,
Through confession of the oneness
Of the Creator of Creation.

I arise to-day
Through the strength of Christ's birth with His
    baptism,
Through the strength of His crucifixion with His
    burial,
Through the strength of His resurrection with His
    ascension,
Through the strength of His descent for the judg-
    ment of Doom.

I arise to-day
Through the strength of the love of Cherubim,
In obedience of angels,
In the service of archangels,
In hope of resurrection to meet with reward.
In prayers of patriarchs,
In predictions of prophets,
In preachings of apostles,
In faiths of confessors,
In innocence of holy virgins,
In deeds of righteous men.

I arise to-day
Through the strength of heaven:
Light of sun
Radiance of moon,
Splendour of fire,
Speed of lightning,
Swiftness of wind,

Depth of sea,
Stability of earth,
Firmness of rock.
I arise to-day
Through God's strength to pilot me:
God's might to uphold me.
God's wisdom to guide me,
God's eye to look before me,
God's ear to hear me,
God's word to speak for me,
God's hand to guard me,
God's way to lie before me,
God's shield to protect me,
God's host to save me
From snares of devils,
From temptations of vices,
From every one who shall wish me ill,
Afar and anear,
Alone and in a multitude. . . .
Christ to shield me to-day
Against poison, against burning,
Against drowning, against wounding,
So that there may come to me abundance of re-
    ward.
Christ with me, Christ before me, Christ behind
    me,
Christ in me, Christ beneath me, Christ above
    me,
Christ on my right, Christ on my left,
Christ when I lie down, Christ when I sit down,
    Christ when I arise,
Christ in the heart of every man who thinks of
    me,
Christ in the mouth of every one who speaks of
    me,

Christ in every eye that sees me,
Christ in every ear that hears me.
I arise to-day
Through a mighty strength, the invocation of the
    Trinity,
Through belief in the threeness,
Through confession of the oneness
Of the Creator of Creation.

Let me know you and love you,
so that I may find my joy in you

Anselm: *Proslogion*

MY SOUL, have you found what you are looking for? You were looking for God, and you
have discovered that he is the supreme being, and
that you could not possibly imagine anything
more perfect. You have discovered that this supreme being is life itself, light, wisdom, goodness,
eternal blessedness and blessed eternity. He is
everywhere, and he is timeless.

Lord my God, you gave me life and restored it
when I lost it. Tell my soul that so longs for you
what else you are besides what it has already
understood, so that it may see you clearly. It
stands on tiptoe to see more, but apart from what
it has seen already, it sees nothing but darkness.
Of course it does not really see darkness, because
there is no darkness in you, but it sees that it can
see no further because of the darkness in itself.

Surely, Lord, inaccessible light is your dwelling place, for no one apart from yourself can
enter into it and fully comprehend you. If I fail
to see this light it is simply because it is too
bright for me. Still, it is by this light that I do

see that I can, even as weak eyes, unable to look straight at the sun, see all that they can by the sun's light.

The light in which you dwell, Lord, is beyond my understanding. It is so brilliant that I cannot bear it, I cannot turn my mind's eye toward it for any length of time. I am dazzled by its brightness, amazed by its grandeur, overwhelmed by its immensity, bewildered by its abundance.

O supreme and inaccessible light, O complete and blessed truth, how far you are from me, even though I am so near to you! How remote you are from my sight, even though I am present to yours! You are everywhere in your entirety, and yet I do not see you; in you I move and have my being, and yet I cannot approach you; you are within me and around me, and yet I do not perceive you.

O God, let me know you and love you so that I may find my joy in you; and if I cannot do so fully in this life, let me at least make some progress every day, until at last that knowledge, love and joy come to me in all their plenitude. While I am here on earth let me learn to know you better, so that in heaven I may know you fully; let my love for you grow deeper here, so that there I may love you fully. On earth then I shall have great joy in hope, and in heaven complete joy in the fulfillment of my hope.

O Lord, through your Son you command us, no, you counsel us to ask, and you promise that you will hear us so that our joy may be complete. Lord, I am making the request that you urge us to make through your Wonder-Counselor. Give me then what you promise to give through your Truth. You, O God, are faithful; grant that I may receive my request, so that my joy may be complete.

Meanwhile, let this hope of mine be in my thoughts and on my tongue; let my heart be filled with it, my voice speak of it; let my soul hunger for it, my body thirst for it, my whole being yearn for it, until I enter into the joy of the Lord, who is Three in One, blessed for ever. Amen.

Incline my heart to your decrees

Robert Bellarmine: *Treatise*

SWEET Lord, *you are meek and merciful.* Who would not give himself wholeheartedly to your service, if he began to taste even a little of your fatherly rule? What command, Lord, do you give your servants? *Take my yoke upon you,* you say. And what is this yoke of yours like? *My yoke,* you say, *is easy and my burden light.* Who would not be glad to bear a yoke that does not press hard but caresses? Who would not be glad for a burden that does not weigh heavy but refreshes? And so you were right to add: *And you will find rest for your souls.* And what is this yoke of yours that does not weary, but gives rest? It is, of course, that first and greatest commandment: *You shall love the Lord your God with all your heart.* What is easier, sweeter, more pleasant, than to love goodness, beauty and love, the fullness of which you are, O Lord, my God?

Is it not true that you promise those who keep your commandments a reward more desirable than great wealth and sweeter than honey? You promise a most abundant reward, for as your apostle James says: *The Lord has prepared a crown of life for those who love him.* What is this crown of life? It is surely a greater good than we can conceive of or desire, as Saint Paul says, quoting Isaiah: *Eye has not seen, ear has not heard, nor has it so much as dawned on man what God has prepared for those who love him.*

The divine plan for the world
is the mirror of the spiritual world
Ephrem: *Sermon*

LORD, shed upon our darkened souls the brilliant light of your wisdom so that we may be enlightened and serve you with renewed purity. Sunrise marks the hour for men to begin their toil, but in our souls, Lord, prepare a dwelling for the day that will never end. Grant that we may come to know the risen life and that nothing may distract us from the delights you offer. Through our unremitting zeal for you, Lord, set upon us the sign of your day that is not measured by the sun.

In your sacrament we daily embrace you and receive you into our bodies; make us worthy to experience the resurrection for which we hope. We have had your treasure hidden within us ever since we received baptismal grace; it grows ever richer at your sacramental table. Teach us to find our joy in your favor! Lord, we have within us your memorial, received at your spiritual table; let us possess it in its full reality when all things shall be made new.

We glimpse the beauty that is laid up for us when we gaze upon the spiritual beauty your immortal will now creates within our mortal selves.

Savior, your crucifixion marked the end of your mortal life; teach us to crucify ourselves and make way for our life in the Spirit. May your resurrection, Jesus, bring true greatness to our spiritual self and may your sacraments be the mirror wherein we may know that self.

Savior, your divine plan for the world is a mirror for the spiritual world; teach us to walk in that world as spiritual men.

Lord, do not deprive our souls of the spiritual vision of you nor our bodies of your warmth and sweetness. The mortality lurking in our bodies spreads corruption through us; may the spiritual waters of your love cleanse the effects of mortality from our hearts. Grant, Lord, that we may hasten to our true city and, like Moses on the mountaintop, possess it now in vision.

A prayer to Christ our Savior

Bridget: *Prayers*

BLESSED are you, my Lord Jesus Christ. You foretold your death and at the Last Supper you marvelously consecrated bread which became your precious body. And then you gave it to your apostles out of love as a memorial of your most holy passion. By washing their feet with your holy hands, you gave them a supreme example of your deep humility.

Honor be to you, my Lord Jesus Christ. Fearing your passion and death, you poured forth blood from your innocent body like sweat, and still you accomplished our redemption as you desired and gave us the clearest proof of your love for all men.

Blessed may you be, my Lord Jesus Christ. After you had been led to Caiaphas, you, the judge of all men, humbly allowed yourself to be handed over to the judgment of Pilate.

Glory be to you, my Lord Jesus Christ, for the mockery you endured when you stood clothed in purple and wearing a crown of sharp thorns. With utmost endurance you allowed vicious men to spit upon your glorious face, blindfold you and beat your cheek and neck with cruelest blows.

Praise be to you, my Lord Jesus Christ. For with the greatest patience you allowed yourself like an innocent lamb to be bound to a pillar and mercilessly scourged, and then to be brought, covered with blood, before the judgment seat of Pilate to be gazed upon by all.

Honor be to you, my Lord Jesus Christ. For after your glorious body was covered with blood, you were condemned to death on the cross, you endured the pain of carrying the cross on your sacred shoulders, and you were led with curses to the place where you were to suffer. Then stripped of your garments, you allowed yourself to be nailed to the wood of the cross.

Everlasting honor be to you, Lord Jesus Christ. You allowed your most holy mother to suffer so much, even though she had never sinned nor ever even consented to the smallest sin. Humbly you looked down upon her with your gentle loving eyes, and to comfort her you entrusted her to the faithful care of your disciple.

Eternal blessing be yours, my Lord Jesus Christ, because in your last agony you held out to all sinners the hope of pardon, when in your mercy you promised the glory of paradise to the penitent thief.

Eternal praise be to you, my Lord Jesus Christ, for the time you endured on the cross the greatest torments and sufferings for us sinners. The sharp pain of your wounds fiercely penetrated even to your blessed soul and cruelly pierced your most sacred heart till finally you sent forth your spirit in peace, bowed your head, and humbly commended yourself into the hands of God your Father, and your whole body remained cold in death.

Blessed may you be, my Lord Jesus Christ. You redeemed our souls with your precious blood and most holy death, and in your mercy you led them from exile back to eternal life.

Blessed may you be, my Lord Jesus Christ. For our salvation you allowed your side and heart to be pierced with a lance; and from that side water and your precious blood flowed out abundantly for our redemption.

Glory be to you, my Lord Jesus Christ. You allowed your blessed body to be taken down from the cross by your friends and laid in the arms of your most sorrowing mother, and you let her wrap your body in a shroud and bury it in a tomb to be guarded by soldiers.

Unending honor be to you, my Lord Jesus Christ. On the third day you rose from the dead and appeared to those you had chosen. And after forty days you ascended into heaven before the eyes of many witnesses, and there in heaven you gathered together in glory those you love, whom you had freed from hell.

Rejoicing and eternal praise be to you, my Lord Jesus Christ, who sent the Holy Spirit into the hearts of your disciples and increased the boundless love of God in their spirits.

Blessed are you and praiseworthy and glorious for ever, my Lord Jesus. You sit upon your throne in your kingdom of heaven, in the glory of your divinity, living in the most holy body you took from a virgin's flesh. So will you appear on that last day to judge the souls of all the living and the dead; you who live and reign with the Father and the Holy Spirit for ever and ever. Amen.

The work of the lay apostle

Decree on the Apostolate of the Laity, nos. 5, 6, 7

CHRIST'S redemptive work, while essentially concerned with the salvation of men, includes also the renewal of the whole temporal order. Hence, the mission of the Church is not only to bring the message and grace of Christ to men but also to penetrate and perfect the temporal order with the spirit of the gospel. . . .

The mission of the Church pertains to the salvation of men, which is to be achieved by belief in Christ and by his grace. The apostolate of the Church and of all its members is primarily designed to manifest Christ's message by words and deeds and to communicate his grace to the world. This is done mainly through the ministry of the Word and the sacraments, entrusted in a special way to the clergy, wherein the laity also have their very important roles to fulfill if they are to be "fellow workers for the truth" (3 Jn 8). It is especially on this level that the apostolate of the laity and the pastoral ministry are mutually complementary.

There are innumerable opportunities open to the laity for the exercise of their apostolate of evangelization and sanctification. The very testimony of their Christian life and good works done in a supernatural spirit have the power to draw men to belief and to God; for the Lord says, "Even so let your light shine before men in order that they may see your good works and give glory to your Father who is in heaven" (Mt 5, 16).

However, an apostolate of this kind does not consist only in the witness of one's way of life; a true apostle looks for opportunities to announce Christ by words addressed either to non-believers with a view to leading them to faith, or to the faithful with a view to instructing, strengthening, and encouraging them to a more fervent life. "For the charity of Christ impels us" (2 Cor. 5, 14). The words of the Apostle should echo in all hearts. "Woe to me if I do not preach the gospel" (1 Cor. 9, 16).

Since, in our own times, new problems are arising and very serious errors are circulating which tend to undermine the foundations of religion, the moral order, and human society itself, this sacred synod earnestly exhorts laymen —each according to his own gifts of intelligence and learning—to be more diligent in doing what they can to explain, defend, and properly apply

Christian principles to the problems of our era in accordance with the mind of the Church. . . .

The laity must take up the renewal of the temporal order as their own special obligation. Led by the light of the gospel and the mind of the Church and motivated by Christian charity, they must act directly and in a definite way in the temporal sphere. As citizens they must cooperate with other citizens with their own particular skill and on their own responsibility. Everywhere and in all things they must seek the justice of God's kingdom.

The temporal order must be renewed in such a way that, without detriment to its own proper laws, it may be brought into conformity with the higher principles of the Christian life and adapted to the shifting circumstances of time, place, and peoples. Preeminent among the works of this type of apostolate is that of Christian social action which the sacred synod desires to see extended to the whole temporal sphere, including culture.

Search for God and realism

Thomas Merton: *Life and Holiness*, pp. 50-51

JOHN Tauler says in one of his sermons that when God is seeking our soul he acts like the woman in the gospel parable, who lost her penny and turned the whole house upside down until she had found it. This "upsetting" of our inner life is essential to spiritual growth, because without it we remain comfortably at rest in more or less illusory ideas of what spiritual perfection really is.

In the doctrine of St. John of the Cross this is described as the "dark night" of passive purification that empties us of our too human concepts of God and of divine things, and leads us into the desert where we are nourished not by bread alone but by the means which can come only directly from him.

Modern theologians have argued at some lengths about the necessity of passive mystical purification for fully mature Christian sanctity. We can here disregard the arguments on either side, since it is enough to say that true sanctity means the full expression of the cross of Christ in our lives, and this cross means the death of what is familiar and normal to us, the death of our everyday selves, in order that we may live on a new level.

And yet, paradoxically, on this new level we recover our old, ordinary selves. It is the familiar self who dies and rises in Christ. The "new man" is totally transformed, and yet he remains the *same person*. He is spiritualized, indeed the Fathers would say he is "divinized" in Christ.

This should warn us that it is useless to cherish "ideals" which, as we imagine, will help us to escape from a self with which we are dissatisfied or disgusted. The way of perfection is not a way of escape. We can only become saints by facing ourselves, by assuming full responsibility for our lives just as they are, with all their handicaps and limitations, and submitting ourselves to the purifying and transforming action of the Savior. . . .

The job of giving ourselves to God and re-
nouncing the world is deeply serious, admitting
of no compromise. It is not enough to meditate
on the way of perfection that includes sacrifice,
prayer, and renunciation of the world. We have
to actually fast, pray, deny ourselves, and become interior men if we are ever going to hear
the voice of God within us.

It is not enough simply to make all perfection
consist in active works, and to say that the obser-
vances and the duties imposed on us by obedience are by themselves sufficient to transform
our whole lives in Christ. The man who simply
"works for" God exteriorly may lack that interior
love for him which is necessary for true perfection. Love seeks not only to serve him but to
know him, to commune with him in prayer, to
abandon itself to him in contemplation.

"O sacred banquet, in which Christ is received, the memory of his Passion is renewed, the mind is filled with grace, and a pledge of future glory is given to us."

THE HOLY EUCHARIST: PRAYERS AND MEDITATIONS

Introduction

"The Holy Eucharist contains the entire spiritual treasury of the Church, that is, Christ himself our passover and living bread. Through his flesh, made living and life-giving by the Holy Spirit, he offers life to men and women, who are thus invited and led to offer themselves, their work, and all creation together with him."

(Decree on the Ministry and Life of Priests, no. 5)

OVER the centuries the Church has prized this great sacrament which has nourished generations of her children. Today the Eucharist is still her most precious possession.

The Eucharist is celebrated primarily at Mass. As the faithful gather together, Jesus Christ comes into their midst, as he promised. (Mt. 18-20) In the words of scripture he speaks to those who are now his own in the world. The priest celebrating the sacrament is another sign of his presence. Above all, Christ comes under the appearance of bread and wine to renew his everlasting covenant with us. The rites and prayers of the Mass are the first guides we should consult to find the treasures contained in this sacrament.

Throughout the centuries, devotion to the Holy Eucharist has taken other forms in the Church, outside of Mass. The sacrament was reserved at first to sustain the sick as "viaticum," as food for their journey. Gradually, other practices of private and public worship of the Sacrament became a vital part of the Church's life. Worship of the Eucharist outside of Mass is still recommended today.

What follows are some aids for public and private worship of the Eucharist outside of Mass. The readings, prayers, reflections and songs may be used for services of Benediction throughout the year, for private meditation, or for those times when Communion is received outside of Mass.

EUCHARISTIC EXPOSITION AND BENEDICTION

Outline of a model service

   a. Exposition — song, incensation

   b. Adoration — reading from scripture
                 — homily, or reading from a church father.
                 — song, silence
                 — intercessions
                 — or part of the Liturgy of the Hours: psalms, reading, canticle, intercessions (cf. pp. 15-127)

   c. Benediction— Eucharistic song (cf. p. 353)
                 — incensation
                 — prayer by the minister (cf. pp. 310-311)
                 — blessing with the Sacrament

   d. Reposition — song.

Some general directions:

1. In arranging Eucharistic services the liturgical seasons should be taken into account. (**Holy Communion and Worship of the Eucharist Outside Mass,** no. 79).

2. When the sacrament is exposed in a monstrance, four to six candles are lighted (no. 93).

3. A single genuflection is made in the presence of the Blessed Sacrament whether reserved in the tabernacle or exposed for public adoration (no. 84).

4. A priest or deacon is ordinarily the minister for exposition of the Eucharist. When they are unavailable, a minister of the Eucharist may expose and repose the sacrament, but not give the blessing (no. 91).

5. The priest or deacon should wear a white cope and humeral veil to give the blessing at the end of adoration, when exposition takes place with the monstrance (no. 92).

TENDERNESS OF GOD
(Advent — Christmas)

HOW could we know of God's gentleness, his tenderness and humility, if Jesus Christ had not come to dwell amongst us? Throughout the ages the human spirit has experienced God's might and power. But a God who is meek and humble? Solely Jesus Christ, God's only Son, could teach us of him.

From his birth in a stable through his long hidden years at Nazareth, our Lord lived among the lowly. Seeking no privilege, he associated with the poor, the sick, the needy and the sinner. The gospel story is filled with their names. All of them found a welcome in the heart of the Lord.

In the Holy Eucharist Jesus Christ still dwells with us. The mystery of Bethlehem and Nazareth, of his ministry to the poor and the needy, continues under the humble signs of bread and wine. No place or person is too small for his care and love. His heart has room for all.

———————

Isaiah 49:13-15

A reading from the book of the prophet Isaiah

Even if a mother forgets her child,
I will never forget you.

Sing out, O heavens, and rejoice, O earth,
   break forth into song, you mountains.
For the Lord comforts his people
   and shows mercy to his afflicted.
But Zion said, "The Lord has forsaken me;
   my Lord has forgotten me."
Can a mother forget her infant,
   be without tenderness for the child of her
     womb?
Even should she forget,
   I will never forget you.

This is the Word of the Lord.

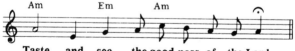

Taste and see the good-ness of the Lord.

Psalm 34:2-3, 4-5, 6-7, 8-9, 17-18, 18, 23

℟. (9) *Taste and see the goodness of the Lord.*
I will bless the Lord at all times;
   his praise shall be ever in my mouth.
Let my soul glory in the Lord;
   the lowly will hear me and be glad.

℟. *Taste and see the goodness of the Lord.*

Glorify the Lord with me,
  let us together extol his name.
I sought the Lord, and he answered me
  and delivered me from all my fears.

℟. *Taste and see the goodness of the Lord.*

Look to him that you may be radiant with joy,
  and your faces may not blush with shame.
When the afflicted man called out, the Lord heard,
  and from all his distress he saved him.

℟. *Taste and see the goodness of the Lord.*

The angel of the Lord encamps
  around those who fear him, and delivers them.
Taste and see how good the Lord is;
  happy the man who takes refuge in him.

℟. *Taste and see the goodness of the Lord.*

The Lord confronts the evildoers,
  to destroy remembrance of them from the
    earth.
When the just cry out, the Lord hears them,
  and from all their distress he rescues them.

℟. *Taste and see the goodness of the Lord.*

The Lord is close to the broken-hearted;
  and those who are crushed in spirit he saves.
The Lord redeems the lives of his servants;
  no one incurs guilt who takes refuge in him.

℟. *Taste and see the goodness of the Lord.*

Matthew 11:25-30

✠ A reading from the holy gospel according
to Matthew

I am meek and humble of heart.

Jesus said: "Father, Lord of heaven and earth,
to you I offer praise; for what you have hidden
from the learned and the clever you have revealed to the merest children. Father, it is true. You
have graciously willed it so. Everything has been
given over to me by my Father. No one knows
the Son but the Father, and no one knows the
Father but the Son—and anyone to whom the
Son wishes to reveal him.

"Come to me, all you who are weary and find
life burdensome, and I will refresh you. Take
my yoke upon your shoulders and learn from
me, for I am gentle and humble of heart. Your
souls will find rest, for my yoke is easy and my
burden light."

This is the gospel of the Lord.

Intercessions

Our Lord Jesus Christ promised to be with
us always. He never forgets his own people. Let
us pray to him and say:
  Lord Jesus, remember us.
Lord Jesus, you are the Word made flesh,
  — we trust in your everlasting love.
In the poverty of a stable you were born to us,
  — bring peace to all the nations of the earth.
In your Epiphany, wise men paid you homage,
  — fill all peoples with your wisdom and knowl-
    edge.

With gentleness and mercy you welcomed sin-
    ners,
— lift the burden of our sins and anxieties.
In this sacrament of your body and blood you
    make a covenant with us,
— renew your people who celebrate the Eucha-
    rist.

PRAYING WITH CHRIST

(Lent)

THROUGHOUT his life, in every circumstance,
    Jesus Christ prayed. In great joy and deepest
sorrow, he sought his Father's will: "Here I am,
Lord, I come to do your will."

Facing the prospect of his Passion in the Garden of Gethsemani, Jesus uttered this same
prayer: "Father, if it is your will, take this cup
from me; yet not my will but yours be done."
Fearful and anxious, he received strength to bear
what would come.

The Holy Eucharist is food that unites us to
Christ and his mysteries. We receive a nourishing
strength to follow him wherever he leads. In this
sacrament Jesus invites us to share his prayer,
making our own the love and devotion he bore
for God, his Father.

We need not be distressed that our frailty
and fears will prevent us from doing God's will.
One stronger than any angel comes to us in this
sacrament. Christ's voice cries out with ours
when we pray, and because of his prayer, the

Father gives us grace to do what we ask: "Thy will be done."

———————

Hebrews 12:18-19, 22-24

A reading from the letter to the Hebrews

You have come to Mount Zion and to the city
of the living God.

You have not drawn near to an untouchable mountain and a blazing fire, nor gloomy darkness and storm and trumpet blast, nor a voice speaking words such that those who heard begged that they be not addressed to them. No, you have drawn near to Mount Zion and the city of the living God, the heavenly Jerusalem, to myriads of angels in festal gathering, to the assembly of the first-born enrolled in heaven, to God the judge of all, to the spirit of just men made perfect, to Jesus, the mediator of a new covenant, and to the sprinkled blood which speaks more eloquently than that of Abel.

This is the Word of the Lord.

Here am I, Lord; I come to do your will.

Psalm 40:2, 4ab, 7-8a, 8b-9, 10

℟. (8.9) *Here am I, Lord; I come to do your will.*

I have waited, waited for the Lord,
    and he stooped toward me and heard my cry.
And he put a new song into my mouth,
    a hymn to our God.

℟. *Here am I, Lord; I come to do your will.*
Sacrifice or oblation you wished not,
   but ears open to obedience you gave me.
Holocausts or sin-offerings you sought not;
   then said I, "Behold, I come.

   ℟. *Here am I, Lord; I come to do your will.*
In the written scroll it is prescribed for me.
To do your will, O my God, is my delight,
   and your law is within my heart!"

   ℟. *Here am I, Lord; I come to do your will.*
I announced your justice in the vast assembly;
   I did not restrain my lips, as you, O Lord,
   know.

   ℟. *Here am I, Lord; I come to do your will.*

Luke 22:39-44

✠ A reading from the holy gospel according
   to Luke

*While he prayed in agony, his sweat became like
drops of blood.*

Jesus went out and made his way, as was his
custom, to the Mount of Olives; his disciples accompanied him. On reaching the place he said to
them, "Pray that you may not be put to the
test." He withdrew from them about a stone's
throw, then went down on his knees and prayed
in these words: "Father, if it is your will, take
this cup from me; yet not my will but yours
be done." An angel then appeared to him from
heaven to strengthen him. In his anguish he
prayed with all the greater intensity, and his

sweat became like drops of blood falling to the ground.

This is the gospel of the Lord.

Intercessions

Our Lord Jesus Christ offered himself in obedience to his Father's will; let us pray to him:
Your will be done, Lord.
Lord Jesus, you called your disciples to follow in your footsteps,
— enlighten our Holy Father, our bishops, and religious leaders as they guide your people.
Lord Jesus, you accepted the cup of suffering and death,
— give strength to the dying to accept the Father's will.
Lord Jesus, in your life and death you acknowledged the wisdom of the Father,
— may all nations submit to the wise rule of God.
Lord Jesus, you gave your Church an example of persevering prayer,
— keep the spirit of prayer strong in us all.
Lord Jesus, you prayed that your disciples might not fail in temptation,
— uphold us when we are tempted.

THE MEMORY OF HIS PASSION
(Lent)

THE Holy Eucharist recalls the Passion of Jesus. Its signs of bread and wine tell of his body given for us, of his blood shed so that our sin might be forgiven. Not merely evoking a memory, the Holy Eucharist makes the Passion of Jesus present for us today. In a mysterious, yet real way, the redeeming love of Jesus Christ is given to all time.

In this sacrament we recall Christ's death. The King of heaven humbled himself to suffer insult, derision and death. Worthy of all honor, he was treated as a fool. A dirty cloak covered his shoulders; a crown of thorns dug deeply into his head. "He was led like a lamb to slaughter and he opened not his mouth."

The memory of the sufferings of Jesus should inspire us to be sensitive to the sufferings of others who now experience humbling, dishonor or pain. Often unnoticed, they wear Christ's crown of thorns and suffer in tragic silence. What we do for them, Jesus accounts as done for himself.

The Holy Eucharist should nourish a deep sense of compassion in the Church. As a memorial of Christ's passion, it impresses this mystery on our minds and hearts, inspiring gratitude for God's love and a desire to serve him in the suffering people of the world.

Revelation 1:5-8

A reading from the book of Revelation

Because he loves us, he has washed away our sins with his blood.

[Grace and peace] from Jesus Christ the faithful witness, the first-born from the dead and ruler of the kings of earth. To him who loves us

and freed us from our sins by his own blood,
who has made us a royal nation of priests in the
service of his God and Father—to him be glory
and power forever and ever! Amen.

See, he comes amid the clouds!
  Every eye shall see him,
  even of those who pierced him.
All the peoples of the earth
  shall lament him bitterly.
  So it is to be! Amen!

The Lord God says, "I am the Alpha and the
Omega, the One who is and who was and who
is to come, the Almighty!"

This is the Word of the Lord.

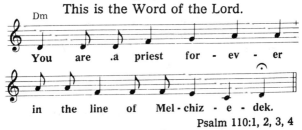

You are a priest for - ev - er
in the line of Mel - chiz - e - dek.

Psalm 110:1, 2, 3, 4

℞. *You are a priest for ever,*
  in the line of Melchizedek.

The Lord said to my Lord: "Sit at my right hand
  till I make your enemies your footstool."

℞. *You are a priest for ever,*
  in the line of Melchizedek.

The scepter of your power the Lord will stretch
  forth from Zion:
  "Rule in the midst of your enemies."

℞. *You are a priest for ever,*
  in the line of Melchizedek.

"Yours is princely power in the day of your birth,
　　in holy splendor;
　before the daystar; like the dew, I have be-
　　gotten you."

　　℟. *You are a priest for ever,*
　　　in the line of Melchizedek.

The Lord has sworn, and he will not repent:
"You are a priest forever, according to the order
　of Melchizedek."

　　℟. *You are a priest for ever,*
　　　in the line of Melchizedek.

Mark 15:16-20

✠ A reading from the holy gospel according
　　to Mark

*They dressed him up in purple and put
a crown of thorns on him.*

The soldiers led Jesus away into the hall
known as the praetorium; at the same time they
assembled the whole cohort. They dressed him
in royal purple, then wove a crown of thorns and
put it on him, and began to salute him, "All
hail! King of the Jews!" Continually striking
Jesus on the head with a reed and spitting at him,
they genuflected before him and pretended to
pay him homage. When they had finished mock-
ing him, they stripped him of the purple, dressed
him in his own clothes, and led him out to crucify
him. This is the gospel of the Lord.

Intercessions

Our Lord Jesus Christ humbled himself even to
　　death on a Cross; let us pray to him and say:
　　Save us by your Cross, Lord.
Lord Jesus, you were dishonored in your Passion,

—may we always honor and recognize the dignity of others.

Lord Jesus, you suffered from the soldiers' cruel blows,

—help all those carrying the wounds of violence and war.

King of heaven, your power extends over all time,

—may all the rulers of the world share your spirit of service.

As our High Priest, you intercede for us with the Father,

—remember our poverty and our needs.

You will come again to judge the living and the dead,

—gather all peoples into your kingdom.

BREAD FOR THE JOURNEY
(Eastertime)

PASSING through the desert, Elijah the prophet appears to be a lonely man in flight. Yet God marks his every step and provides bread for his journey.

The two disciples on the way to Emmaus appear to be alone in their disappointment. But they too are accompanied. Though they are hardly aware of him, Jesus Christ journeys with them. Gradually they experience his burning strength. Finally, they recognize him "in the breaking of the bread."

"How slow you are to believe!" Jesus tells them. Yet, while chiding them for their lack of faith, he never abandons them or speaks faster than they can think.

Neither is our life journey unaccompanied. God walks with us step by step. The Holy Eucharist is a sign of his providential care, whereby he speaks his truth within our hearts patiently and constantly. "He disappeared from before their eyes that they might find him in their hearts," St. Augustine says of the disciples. In the Holy Eucharist God signifies his desire for this final resting place where he wishes to be found—the human heart.

————————

1 Kings 19:4-8

A reading from the first book of Kings

In the strength of that food, Elijah walked
to the mountain of God.

Elijah went a day's journey into the desert, until he came to a broom tree and sat beneath it. He prayed for death: "This is enough, O Lord! Take my life, for I am no better than my fathers." He lay down and fell asleep under the broom tree, but then an angel touched him and ordered him to get up and eat. He looked and there at his head was a hearth cake and a jug of water. After he ate and drank, he lay down again, but the angel of the Lord came back a second time, touched him, and ordered, "Get up and eat, else the journey will be too long for you!" He got up, ate and drank; then, strengthened by that food, he walked forty days and forty nights to the mountain of God, Horeb.

This is the Word of the Lord.

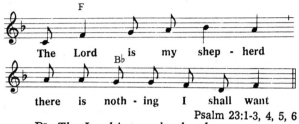

The Lord is my shepherd
there is noth-ing I shall want
Psalm 23:1-3, 4, 5, 6

℟. *The Lord is my shepherd;*
there is nothing I shall want.

The Lord is my shepherd; I shall not want.
  In verdant pastures he gives me repose;
Beside restful waters he leads me;
  he refreshes my soul.
He guides me in right paths
  for his name's sake.

    ℟. *The Lord is my shepherd;*
    there is nothing I shall want.

Even though I walk in the dark valley
  I fear no evil; for you are at my side
With your rod and your staff
  that give me courage.

    ℟. *The Lord is my shepherd;*
    there is nothing I shall want.

You spread the table before me
  in the sight of my foes;
You anoint my head with oil;
  my cup overflows.

    ℟. *The Lord is my shepherd;*
    there is nothing I shall want.

Only goodness and kindness follow me
  all the days of my life;
And I shall dwell in the house of the Lord
  for years to come.

℟. *The Lord is my shepherd;*
there is nothing I shall want.

Luke 24:13-35

✠ A reading from the holy gospel according
to Luke

They recognized the Lord when he broke
the bread with them.

Two of the disciples of Jesus that same day
[the first of the week] were making their way to
a village named Emmaus seven miles distant
from Jerusalem, discussing as they went all that
had happened. In the course of their lively ex-
change, Jesus approached and began to walk
along with them. However they were restrained
from recognizing him. He said to them, "What
are you discussing as you go your way?" They
halted in distress and one of them, Cleopas by
name, asked him, "Are you the only resident of
Jerusalem who does not know the things that
went on there these past few days?" He said to
them, "What things?"

They said: "All those that had to do with Jesus
of Nazareth, a prophet powerful in word and
deed in the eyes of God and all the people; how
our chief priests and leaders delivered him up
to be condemned to death, and crucified him. We
were hoping that he was the one who would set
Israel free. Besides all this, today, the third day
since these things happened, some women of our
group have just brought us some astonishing
news. They were at the tomb before dawn and
failed to find his body, but returned with the tale
that they had seen a vision of angels who declared he was alive. Some of our number went to

the tomb and found it to be just as the women said; but him they did not see."

Then he said to them, "What little sense you have! How slow you are to believe all that the prophets have announced! Did not the Messiah have to undergo all this so as to enter into his glory?" Beginning, then, with Moses and all the prophets, he interpreted for them every passage of Scripture which referred to him. By now they were near the village to which they were going, and he acted as if he were going farther. But they pressed him: "Stay with us. It is nearly evening—the day is practically over." So he went in to stay with them.

When he had seated himself with them to eat, he took bread, pronounced the blessing, then broke the bread and began to distribute it to them. With that their eyes were opened and they recognized him; whereupon he vanished from their sight. They said to one another, "Were not our hearts burning inside us as he talked to us on the road and explained the Scriptures to us?"

They got up immediately and returned to Jerusalem, where they found the Eleven and the rest of the company assembled. They were greeted with, "The Lord has been raised! It is true! He has appeared to Simon." Then they recounted what had happened on the road and how they had come to know him in the breaking of the bread.   This is the gospel of the Lord.

Intercessions

Our Lord Jesus Christ journeyed with his disciples and lifted up their hearts; let us say to him:

Lord, stay always with us.
As you opened the scriptures to your disciples
   on the way to Emmaus,
—teach your Church the words of life.
Lord Jesus, you bore patiently with your disciples' slowness,
—be patient with us who wish to follow you.
At table you revealed yourself in the breaking of
   the bread,
—in the Sacrament of the Eucharist reveal yourself to us.
Your disciples hastened to announce your resurrection,
—may we share your risen life with all we meet.

HIS GRACE IS POURED OUT
(Pentecost)

THE Passion of Christ, according to St. John's
   gospel, is pervaded with ironic hints of God's
wisdom and power. Those who crucified Jesus
saw only his defeat and death. Yet they were
fulfilling a plan for the world's salvation. In his
darkest hours, the glory of God shines forth
from the suffering Christ.

When the soldiers pierced the side of Jesus,
they were carrying out a routine distasteful task.
Another man had to be killed, and quickly, lest
the coming feast be spoiled by the sight of death
in the land.

According to God's purposes, however, the
earth was blessed as blood and water from the
heart of Jesus fell to the ground. At that moment he gave the world his Spirit for its new life.

The Eucharist is a sign of God's eternal covenant of mercy with us. His grace is still quietly poured out; the world is blessed, though hardly aware of what it receives. Day after day, with unwearied love, the heart of Jesus is opened and his Spirit freshly given to us.

----

1 John 5:4-7a, 8b

A reading from the first letter of John

There are three witnesses the Spirit and the water and the blood.

Everyone begotten of God conquers the world,
and the power that has conquered the world
is this faith of ours.
Who, then, is conqueror of the world?
The one who believes that Jesus is the Son of
    God.
Jesus Christ it is who came through water and
blood—
not in water only,
but in the water and blood.
It is the Spirit who testifies to this,
and the Spirit is truth.
Thus there are three that testify,
and these three are of one accord.

This is the Word of the Lord.

I will take the cup of sal - va - tion and call on the name of the Lord.

Psalm 116:12-13, 15-16, 17-18

℟. *I will take the cup of salvation, and call*
  on the name of the Lord.

How shall I make a return to the Lord
  for all the good he has done for me?
The cup of salvation I will take up,
  and I will call upon the name of the Lord.

℟. *I will take the cup of salvation, and call*
  on the name of the Lord.

Precious in the eyes of the Lord
  is the death of his faithful ones.
O Lord, I am your servant, the son of your hand-
    maid;
  you have loosed my bonds.

℟. *I will take the cup of salvation, and call*
  on the name of the Lord.

To you will I offer sacrifice of thanksgiving,
  and I will call upon the name of the Lord.
My vows to the Lord I will pay
  in the presence of all his people.

℟. *I will take the cup of salvation, and call*
  on the name of the Lord.

John 19:31-37

✠ A reading from the holy gospel according
      to John

When they pierced his side with a spear,
blood and water flowed out.

Since it was the Preparation Day the Jews did
not want to have the bodies left on the cross
during the sabbath, for that sabbath was a solemn feast day. They asked Pilate that the legs be

broken and the bodies be taken away. According
ly, the soldiers came and broke the legs of the
men crucified with Jesus, first of the one, then
of the other. When they came to Jesus and saw
that he was already dead, they did not break his
legs. One of the soldiers thrust a lance into his
side, and immediately blood and water flowed
out. (This testimony has been given by an eye-
witness, and his testimony is true. He tells what
he knows is true, so that you may believe.) These
events took place for the fulfillment of Scripture:

"Break none of his bones."

There is still another Scripture passage which
says:

"They shall look on him whom they have
pierced."

This is the gospel of the Lord.

Intercessions

Let us pray to our Lord Jesus Christ whose side
was pierced by a soldier's lance and say to him:
Lord Jesus, give us your Spirit.
Your mother Mary and beloved disciple John
stood beneath your Cross,
— keep the memory of your Passion and Death
always in your Church.
You removed the curse of sin and death by your
Cross,
— bless all the peoples of the earth with new life.
From your open side blood and water flowed,
— enrich your Church with the Sacraments of
Baptism and the Eucharist.

From the Cross you bestowed your Holy Spirit,
— by this same Spirit renew the face of the
earth.

AND HE SHALL FEED HIS FLOCK

LIKE the Jews of old who followed Moses, a
multitude of people followed Jesus Christ to
a desert place one day. With food in small supply they were hungry; so he provided them with
a nourishing bread. His gift foretold a Bread he
would multiply to feed generations—a Living
Bread, the Holy Eucharist.

The gospel story of the miracle of the loaves
provides a wealth of teaching on the Holy Eucharist.

In this sacrament Jesus Christ is present as our
compassionate Lord who cares for a people he
calls his own. Having shared the weariness of
our life's journey, he knows our hunger and
thirst. He also sees our resources in short supply.

Listen carefully to the questions he asks his
disciples in the desert. "How many loaves do you
have? Go and see." They bring their few loaves
and fish; only then does he multiply them for
distribution.

"How many loaves do you have? Go and see."
Fascinated by the miraculous multiplication, we
scarcely notice the vital collaboration of the disciples in the story. They must discover first what
they have and generously bring it, little as it is,
to be multiplied by divine power. God always

waits for the human heart to offer what gifts it can.

In the Holy Eucharist Jesus Christ accompanies us on our life journey, even to its desert places. As we go through life we cry out from our fears and inadequacy "We haven't enough!" Not enough strength, or courage, or wisdom, or faith. Our resources are too small and famine seems at hand.

"What do you have? Go and see," the Lord says. Do, give, think, bring all you can. And as we do, a Living Bread is given to us, a "bread of the mighty," a "Bread from heaven"—and we have more than enough to call our own.

———————

Exodus 16:2-4, 12-15

A reading from the book of Exodus

The Lord will rain bread on us from heaven.

In the desert the whole Israelite community grumbled against Moses and Aaron. The Israelites said to them, "Would that we had died at the Lord's hand in the land of Egypt, as we sat by our fleshpots and ate our fill of bread! But you had to lead us into this desert to make the whole community die of famine!"

Then the Lord said to Moses, "I will now rain down bread from heaven for you. Each day the people are to go out and gather their daily portion; thus will I test them, to see whether they follow my instructions or not. I have heard the grumbling of the Israelites. Tell them: In the evening twilight you shall eat flesh, and in the morning you shall have your fill of bread, so that you may know that I, the Lord, am your God."

In the evening quail came up and covered the camp. In the morning a dew lay all about the lamp, and when the dew evaporated, there on the surface of the desert were fine flakes like hoarfrost on the ground. On seeing it, the Israelites asked one another, "What is this?" for they did not know what it was. But Moses told them, "This is the bread which the Lord has given you to eat."

This is the Word of the Lord.

The Lord gave them bread from heav-en.

Psalm 78:3-4a, 7ab, 23-24, 25 and 54

℟. (24) *The Lord gave them bread from heaven.*

What we have heard and know,
    and what our fathers have declared to us,
We will not hide from their sons;
    we will declare to the generations to come,
That they should put their hope in God,
    and not forget the deeds of God.

℟. *The Lord gave them bread from heaven.*

He commanded the skies above
    and the doors of heaven he opened;
He rained manna upon them for food
    and gave them heavenly bread.

℞. *The Lord gave them bread from heaven.*
The bread of the mighty was eaten by men;
    even a surfeit of provisions he sent them.
And he brought them to his holy land,
    to the mountains his right hand had won.

℞. *The Lord gave them bread from heaven.*

Mark 6:34-44

✠ A reading from the holy gospel according
        to Luke

Jesus Feeds Five Thousand

Upon disembarking Jesus saw a vast crowd. He pitied them, for they were like sheep without a shepherd; and he began to teach them at great length. It was now getting late and his disciples came to him with a suggestion: "This is a deserted place and it is already late. Why do you not dismiss them so that they can go to the crossroads and villages around here and buy themselves something to eat?" "You give them something to eat," Jesus replied. At that they said, "Are we to go and spend two hundred days' wages for bread to feed them?" "How many loaves have you?" Jesus asked. "Go and see." When they learned the number they answered, "Five, and two fish." He told them to make the people sit down on the green grass in groups or parties.

The people took their places in hundreds and fifties, neatly arranged like flower beds. Then, taking the five loaves and the two fish, Jesus raised his eyes to heaven, pronounced a blessing, broke the loaves, and gave them to the disciples to distribute. He divided the two fish among all of them and they ate until they had their fill. They gathered up enough leftovers to fill twelve baskets, besides what remained of the fish. Those who had eaten the loaves numbered five thousand men.

Intercessions

Our Lord Jesus Christ fed our ancestors in the desert; let us pray to him and say:
> *Lord Jesus, strengthen us.*

Lord Jesus, you asked your disciples to give of what they had,
— may we give you everything we possess.

In this sacrament you offer us abundant gifts,
— open the treasures of your heart to all peoples.

As you fed those who came to you hungry and in need,
— inspire us to assist our brothers and sisters.

Your Church is a sign of your love in this world,
— may she always be concerned for the poor.

You know the hunger and weariness of the human heart,
— help those who have reached an end to their endurance.

THIS IS MY BODY

WHEN Jesus Christ entered the supper room to eat the Passover meal with his disciples, he faced a critical situation. Powerful forces were drawn up against him, ready to take his life. His enemies were moving to stop him.

At his side were his disciples, "his own who were in the world." They gave him little support, however, for they were arguing among themselves. Not only did Jesus face their pettiness that evening, but more strongly he sensed their impending betrayal of him.

What would he do? He might respond, understandably, with caution and draw back. Like the servant, whom the prophet described, he might well say, "I thought I had toiled in vain; and for nothing, uselessly, spent my strength. . ." (Is 49).

Jesus, however, took bread and gave it to his disciples. "Take this," he said, "this is my body." He took the cup and gave it to them. "This is my blood, the blood of my new covenant, to be poured out in behalf of many."

That night, which seemed to call for wariness and regret, Jesus gave himself in love to his Father and to his disciples. As Savior and Redeemer he gave himself unhesitatingly for the life of the world.

The Holy Eucharist makes a supper room of every time and place. Until the end of time, Jesus Christ will offer his body and blood for all.

Exodus 12:21-27

A reading from the book of Exodus

When the Lord sees the blood on the door, he will pass over your home.

Moses called all the elders of Israel and said to them, "Go and procure lambs for your families, and slaughter them as Passover victims.

Then take a bunch of hyssop, and dipping it in the blood that is in the basin, sprinkle the lintel and the two doorposts with this blood. But none of you shall go outdoors until morning. For the Lord will go by, striking down the Egyptians. Seeing the blood on the lintel and the two doorposts, the Lord will pass over that door and not let the destroyer come into your houses to strike you down.

"You shall observe this as a perpetual ordinance for yourselves and your descendants. Thus, you must also observe this rite when you have entered the land which the Lord will give you as he promised. When your children ask you, 'What does this rite of yours mean?' you shall reply, 'This is the Passover sacrifice of the Lord, who passed over the houses of the Israelites in Egypt; when he struck down the Egyptians, he spared our houses.'"

Then the people bowed down in worship.

This is the Word of the Lord.

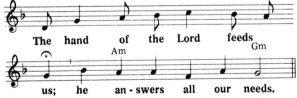

The hand of the Lord feeds us; he an-swers all our needs.

Psalm 145:10-11, 15-16, 17-18

℟. (16) *The hand of the Lord feeds us; he answers all our needs.*

Let all your works give thanks, O Lord, and let your faithful ones bless you.

Let them discourse of the glory of your kingdom
　　and speak of your might.

　　℞. *The hand of the Lord feeds us;*
　　　he answers all our needs.

The eyes of all look hopefully to you,
　　and you give them their food in due season;
You open your hand
　　and satisfy the desire of every living thing.

　　℞. *The hand of the Lord feeds us;*
　　　he answers all our needs.

The Lord is just in all his ways
　　and holy in all his works.
The Lord is near to all who call upon him,
　　to all who call upon him in truth.

　　℞. *The hand of the Lord feeds us;*
　　　he answers all our needs.

Mark 14:12-16, 22-26

✠ A reading from the holy gospel
according to Mark
This is my body. This is my blood.

On the first day of Unleavened Bread, when it
was customary to sacrifice the paschal lamb, his
disciples said to Jesus, "Where do you wish us
to go to prepare the Passover supper for you?"
He sent two of his disciples with these instructions: "Go into the city and you will come upon
a man carrying a water jar. Follow him. Whatever house he enters, say to the owner, 'The
Teacher asks, Where is my guest room where I
may eat the Passover with my disciples?' Then
he will show you an upstairs room, spacious,
furnished, and all in order. That is the place you
are to get ready for us." The disciples went off.

When they reached the city they found it just as he had told them, and they prepared the Passover supper.

During the meal he took bread, blessed and broke it, and gave it to them. "Take this," he said, "this is my body." He likewise took a cup, gave thanks and passed it to them, and they all drank from it. He said to them: 'This is my blood, the blood of the covenant, to be poured out on behalf of many. I solemnly assure you, I will never again drink the fruit of the vine until the day when I drink it new in the reign of God."

After singing songs of praise, they walked out to the Mount of Olives.

This is the gospel of the Lord.

Intercessions

Our Lord Jesus Christ has saved us from our
    sins. Let us pray to him and say:
    You are the Savior of the world.
Lord Jesus, you celebrated the Passover with
    your disciples,
—free us from the slavery of our sins.
You were not overcome by the power of evil,
—deliver us from the forces of darkness and
    death.
In love you gave yourself for the life of the world,
—enable us to give ourselves generously to our
    brothers and sisters.
You wished to be united to those who were your
    own in this world,
—unite all the families, churches, and nations of
    the world.

PLEDGE OF THE WORLD TO COME

THE Holy Eucharist contains a promise of the future as well as a remembrance of God's graciousness in the past. Jesus assures us that, if we partake of the living bread come down from heaven, we will have life everlasting. Death itself cannot put aside this promise made by the Word of God. We will rise again.

"The slip of a vine planted in the ground bears fruits at the proper time. The grain of wheat falls into the ground and decays only to be raised up again and multiplied by the Spirit of God who sustains all things. . . . In the same way our bodies, which have been nourished by the eucharist, will be buried in the earth and will decay, but they will rise again at the appointed time, for the Word of God will raise them up to the glory of God the Father" (St. Irenaeus).

Not only are we promised a personal resurrection, but we will share God's glory with others. This Bread, which has fed generations, will unite generations for an unending feast. Besides the company of the Virgin Mary and all the saints, we will enjoy reunion with our families and friends who have gone before us into our heavenly inheritance.

The Eucharist is a foretaste of the world to come.

Deuteronomy 8:2-3, 15b-16a

A reading from the book of Deuteronomy

He gave you food finer than any you have ever known.

Moses said to the people: "Remember how for forty years now the Lord, your God, has directed all your journeying in the desert, so as to test you by affliction and find out whether or not it was your intention to keep his commandments. He therefore let you be afflicted with hunger, and then fed you with manna, a food unknown to you and your fathers, in order to show you that not by bread alone does man live, but by every word that comes forth from the mouth of the Lord.

"Remember the Lord, your God, who brought forth water for you from the flinty rock and fed you in the desert with manna, a food unknown to your fathers."

This is the Word of the Lord.

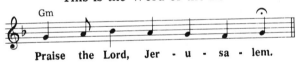

Praise the Lord, Jer - u - sa - lem.

Psalm 147:12-13, 14-15, 19-20

℟. (12a) *Praise the Lord, Jerusalem.*

Glorify the Lord, O Jerusalem;
    praise your God, O Zion.
For he has strengthened the bars of your gates,
    he has blessed your children within you.

℟. *Praise the Lord, Jerusalem.*

He has granted peace in your borders;
    with the best of wheat he fills you.

He sends forth his command to the earth;
   and swiftly runs his word!

  ℟. *Praise the Lord, Jerusalem.*

He has proclaimed his word to Jacob,
   his statutes and his ordinances to Israel.
He has not done thus for any other nation;
   his ordinances he has not made known to
   them. Alleluia.

  ℟. *Praise the Lord, Jerusalem.*

John 6:51-58

✠ A reading from the holy gospel
according to John

My flesh and blood are true food and drink.

Jesus said to the crowd of the Jews:
   "I myself am the living bread
   come down from heaven.
   If anyone eats this bread
   he shall live forever;
   the bread I will give
   is my flesh for the life of the world."
At this the Jews quarreled among themselves,
saying, "How can he give us his flesh to eat?"
Thereupon Jesus said to them:
   "Let me solemnly assure you,
   if you do not eat the flesh of the Son of Man
   and drink his blood,
   you have no life in you.
   He who feeds on my flesh
   and drinks my blood
   has life eternal,
   and I will raise him up on the last day.

For my flesh is real food
and my blood real drink.
The man who feeds on my flesh
and drinks my blood
remains in me, and I in him.
Just as the Father who has life sent me
and I have life because of the Father,
so the man who feeds on me
will have life because of me.
This is the bread that came down from heaven.
Unlike your ancestors who ate and died none-
theless,
the man who feeds on this bread shall live forever."
This is the gospel of the Lord.

Intercessions

Our Lord Jesus Christ has promised life everlasting; let us pray to him and say:
Lord, grant us eternal life.
Lord Jesus, you came into the world as the
Bread from heaven,
— bestow on the nations of the earth hope in the
world to come.
With words of faith, you answered the doubts
of your disciples,
— may we not waver in our faith in you.
Rising to new life, you destroyed the power of
death,
— at our death, raise us up again.
Lord Jesus, you promised paradise to the repentant thief,
— grant forgiveness and new life to sinners.

You raised Lazarus, your friend, from the tomb
— give unending light and peace to our families
and friends who have died.

PRAYERS

LORD Jesus Christ,
   you gave us the eucharist
as the memorial of your suffering and death.
May our worship of this sacrament of your body
   and blood
help us to experience the salvation you won for
   us
and the peace of the kingdom
where you live with the Father and the Holy
   Spirit,
one God, for ever and ever. ℟. **Amen.**

Lord our God,
in this great sacrament
we come into the presence of Jesus Christ, your
   Son,
born of the Virgin Mary
and crucified for our salvation.
May we who declare our faith in this fountain of
   love and mercy
drink from it the water of everlasting life.
We ask this through Christ our Lord. ℟. **Amen.**

Lord our God,
may we always give due honor
to the sacramental presence of the Lamb who
   was slain for us.
May our faith be rewarded

by the vision of his glory,
who lives and reigns for ever and ever. ℞. **Amen.**

Lord our God,
you have given us the true bread from heaven.
In the strength of this food
may we live always by your life
and rise in glory on the last day.

We ask this through Christ our Lord. ℞. **Amen.**

Lord,
give to our hearts
the light of faith and the fire of love,
that we may worship in spirit and in truth
our God and Lord, present in this sacrament,
who lives and reigns for ever and ever. ℞. **Amen.**

Lord,
may this sacrament of new life
warm our hearts with your love
and make us eager
for the eternal joy of your kingdom.

We ask this through Christ our Lord. ℞. **Amen.**

Lord our God,
teach us to cherish in our hearts
the paschal mystery of your Son
by which you redeemed the world.
Watch over the gifts of grace
your love has given us
and bring them to fulfillment
in the glory of heaven.

We ask this through Christ our Lord. ℞. **Amen.**

READINGS ON THE HOLY EUCHARIST

The mystery of faith

Paul VI: *Address of March 28, 1970.*

IS THE sacrament of the Eucharist hard to understand? Yes, it is hard, because it is a matter of something real and most unique which is accomplished by the divine power and which surpasses our normal natural capacity to comprehend. We have to believe it, on Christ's word; it is "the mystery of faith" par excellence.

But, let us be careful. In this sacrament the Lord presents himself to us not as he is but as he wishes us to consider him, as he wishes us to approach him. He offers himself to us under the aspect of expressive signs which he himself chose. It is as if he said: Look at me in this way, get to know me like this. The signs of the bread and wine are to tell you what I wish to be for you. He speaks to us by means of these signs, and says: This is how I am among you now.

Therefore, though we cannot enjoy his tangible presence, we can and ought to enjoy his real presence, under these significant forms. What is Jesus' intention in giving himself to us in the Eucharist? If we think about it well, we shall see that his intention is most patent! It tells us many, many things about Jesus. Above all, it tells us about his love. It tells us that he, Jesus, though he conceals himself in the Eucharist, also reveals himself in it, reveals himself in love. The "mystery of faith" opens up as the "mystery of love." Think of it: this is the sacramental garb which at the same time hides and reveals Jesus: bread and wine, given for us.

Jesus gives himself; presents himself. This is the center, the focal point of the whole of the gospel, of the Incarnation, of the Redemption. . . Born for us, given for us.

For each of us? Yes, for each of us. Jesus has multiplied his real but sacramental presence in time and number, in order to be able to offer each of us—we mean each of us—the good fortune, the joy to approach him, and to be able to say: He is for me, he is mine. "[He] loved me," St. Paul says, "and gave himself for me" (Gal 2:20).

And for all, too? Yes, for all. This is another aspect of Jesus' love which is expressed in the Eucharist. You know the words with which Jesus instituted this sacrament and which the priest repeats in the consecration at Mass: "eat, *all* of you; drink, *all of you* . . . ." For this same sacrament was instituted during an evening meal, a familiar and ordinary occasion and means of coming together, of being united. The Eucharist is the sacrament which represents and produces the unity of Christians. This aspect of it is very dear to the Church and is highly valued today.

For example, the recent Council used the following extremely meaningful words about it: Christ "instituted in his Church the wonderful sacrament of the Eucharist by which the unity of the Church is both signified and effected."

Offering ourselves in union with Christ to the Father

Columba Marmion: *Christ the Life of the Soul,*
pp. 256-257

WE MUST be united to Christ in his immolation and offer ourselves with him; then he takes us with him, he immolates us with him, he bears us before his Father, in the odor of sweetness. It is ourselves we must offer with Jesus Christ. If the faithful share, through baptism, in the priesthood of Christ, it is, says St. Peter, that they may "offer up spiritual sacrifices, acceptable to God through Jesus Christ" (1 Pt 2:5).

This is so true that in more than one prayer following the offering about to be made to God, the Church, while awaiting the moment of the consecration, lays stress on this union of our sacrifice with that of her Bridegroom. "Vouchsafe, O Lord," she says, to sanctify these gifts, and receiving the oblation of this spiritual victim, make *us* an eternal sacrifice to yourself."

But in order for us to be thus accepted by God, the offering of ourselves must be united to the offering Christ made of himself upon the cross and renews upon the altar. Our Lord substituted himself for us in his immolation, he took the place of us all, and that is why when he died we, in principle, died with him: "Since one died for all, therefore all died" (2 Cor 5:14). For this mystical death to take place effectually in each one of us, we must unite ourselves to his sacrifice on the altar.

And how are we to unite ourselves to Christ Jesus in this character of victim? By yielding ourselves, like him, to the entire accomplishment of the divine good pleasure.

It is for God to fully dispose of the victim offered to him; we must be in this essential attitude of giving *all* to God, of making our acts of self-renunciation and mortification, of accepting the sufferings and trials of each day for love of him, so that we may be able to say, like Jesus Christ at the moment of his Passion: "I do this, that the world may know that I love the Father" (Jn 14: 31)—that is, to offer ourselves with Jesus.

Let us offer the divine Son of his eternal Father and offer ourselves with this "holy Host" in the same dispositions that animated the Sacred Heart of Christ upon the cross: intense love of his Father and of our brethren, ardent desire for the salvation of souls, and full abandonment to all that is willed from on high, above all, if it contains what is painful and vexatious for our nature. When we do this, we offer God the most acceptable homage he can receive from us.

We herein have also the most certain means of being transformed into Jesus, especially if we unite ourselves to him in Communion, which is the most fruitful partaking of the Sacrifice of the Altar; for, if we are united to Christ he immolates us with him, renders us pleasing to his Father and makes us, by his grace, more and more like to himself.

The Eucharist and brotherhood

John Chrysostom: *Homily 8 on the Epistle to the Romans*

"WHERE two or three are gathered in my name there am I in their midst" (Mt 18:20). It is, indeed, proper to a great and strong friendship that it maintains unity among those who love one another. "Are there people so wretched," I hear you say, "that they do not desire to have Christ in their midst?"

There certainly are—we who fight one another. Perhaps you will object scornfully: "What are you saying? Don't you see that we are all within the same walls, within the same church, unanimous in the same fold, without the slightest dissension, crying in unison under the leadership of the same shepherd, listening together to what is said, and praying in common? And you talk about fights and discords!"

Yes, I speak about fights, and I am neither mad nor misled. I see what I see, and I know that we are in the same fold and under the same shepherd. And that is why I deplore so much more that in spite of all these signs of togetherness, we are divided. "But," you will say, "tell us what division there is among ourselves?" Here there is none, but as soon as your meeting is over, one starts criticizing another; one publicly harms another; one is devoured by envy, by avarice or cupidity; another practices violence, another abandons himself to sensuality, yields to deceit or fraud. If your souls could be stripped naked, you would realize that I am right in all that I am saying and you would recognize that I am not mad. . . .

You will say, "We are not doing that sort of thing to harm others but to protect ourselves." It is this precisely that grieves me: living among brothers, we feel it necessary to be on our guard lest someone harm us, and we feel we must take so many precautions. The cause of all this is frequent lying and trickery, a great weakening of charity, and constant quarrels. Hence, there are a good number of people who have more trust in pagans than in Christians. Surely, this is a source of confusion, tears, and sighs.

Therefore, respect that Table in which we all participate. Respect Christ immolated for us. Respect the sacrifice that is offered. After participating in such a Table, and communing such Food, why take up arms against one another when we should all together be armed against the devil? It is this which makes us weak. Far from gathering all our shields on one common front against him, we unite to fight our brothers; we line up under his command instead of fighting against him. Let us repeat: we aim our arrows at our brothers. "What arrows?" you ask. The arrows of tongue and lips. Not only arrows and javelins cause wounds. Certain words inflict more profound wounds.

How can we put an end to this kind of war? By reflecting that a word pronounced against your brother is a poison shot from your mouth, and that calumnies affect a member of Christ. "But," you reply, "I have been insulted." If your neighbor had harmed you, ask God to show mercy to him. He is your brother, one of his members. He is called to one same Table with you.

They came "to know him in the breaking of bread"

Gregory the Great: *Homily 23*

TWO disciples were walking together. They did not believe, yet they were talking about Jesus. Suddenly, he appeared, but under characteristics which they could not recognize. To their bodily eyes the Lord thus manifested externally what was taking place in their innermost depths, in the thoughts of their heart. The disciples were inwardly divided between love and doubt. The Lord was really present at their side, but he did not let himself be recognized. He offered his presence to these men who spoke of him, but because they doubted him he hid his true visage from them. He spoke to them and reproached them for their little sense. He interpreted for them every passage of Scripture which referred to him, but since he was still a stranger to the faith of their heart he acted as if he were going farther. . . .

In acting in such a manner, the Truth who is sincere was not being deceitful: he was showing himself to the eyes of his disciples as he appeared in their minds. And the Lord wished to see whether these disciples, who did not yet love him as God, would at least be friendly to him under the guise of a stranger. But those with whom Truth walked could not have been far from charity; they invited him to share their lodging, as one does with a traveler. Can we say simply that they invited him? The Scripture says that "they pressed him" (Lk 24:29). It shows us by this example that when we invite strangers under our roof, our invitation must be a pressing one.

They thus set the table, serve the food, and in the breaking of bread discover the God whom they had failed to come to know in the explanation of the Scriptures. It was not in hearing the precepts of God that they were enlightened, but in carrying them out: "It is not those who hear the law who are just in the sight of God; it is those who keep it who will be declared just" (Rom 2:13). If anyone wishes to understand what he has heard, let him hasten to put into practice whatever he has grasped. The Lord was not recognized while he was speaking; he was pleased to make himself known while he was offered something to eat. Let us then, beloved brothers, love to practice charity. It is of this that Paul speaks to us: "Love your fellow Christians always. Do not neglect to show hospitality, for by that means some have entertained angels without knowing it" (Heb 3:1-2). Peter also says: "Be mutually hospitable without complaining" (1 Pt 4:9). And Truth himself speaks to us of it: "I was a stranger and you welcomed me" (Mt 25:35). . . . "As often as you did it for one of my least brothers," the Lord will declare on the day of judgment, "you did it for me" (Mt 25: 40). . . .

Despite this, we are so slothful in the face of the grace of hospitality! Let us, my brothers, appreciate the greatness of this virtue. Let us receive Christ at our table so as to be welcomed at his eternal supper. Let us show hospitality to Christ present in the stranger now so that at the judgment he will not ignore us as strangers but will welcome us as brothers into his Kingdom.

The Names of the Eucharist

Catechism of the Council of Trent.

SINCE it is impossible to express the excellence of the Sacrament of the Eucharist in one word, many words have been used to describe it.

Sometimes it is called "Eucharist," a word that can mean either "good grace" or "thanksgiving." Surely it is a "good grace" because it signifies eternal life, as Scripture says, "The grace of God is eternal life." It also contains Christ the Lord who is the true grace and fountain of all graces.

We can call it also "thanksgiving," for when we sacrifice this purest Victim we give infinite thanks daily to God for his kindness to us, especially for the gift of grace he grants us in this Sacrament. According to the Scripture "thanksgiving" recalls what Christ the Lord did at the institution of this mystery: "Then, taking bread and giving thanks, he broke it and gave it to them." . . .

Frequently the Sacrament is called "Sacrifice," for it was instituted by Christ for two purposes: one, that it might be the heavenly food for our souls, and the other, that the Church might have a perpetual sacrifice, by which our sins might be expiated and our heavenly Father, offended by our crimes, might be turned from wrath to mercy. The Paschal Lamb, offered and eaten by the children of Israel as a sacrament and a sacrifice, is a type of this.

It is called also "Communion," a term taken from the Apostle Paul. "Is not the cup of blessing we bless a communion in the blood of Christ? And is not the bread we break a communion in the body of Christ? Because the loaf is one, we, many though we are, are one body, for we all partake of the one loaf." As St. John Damascene explains, this Sacrament unites us to Christ, makes us partakers of his flesh and divinity, reconciles and unites us to one another in the same Christ, and forms us, as it were, into one body.

In this same sense, it is called a "Sacrament of peace and love." They are unworthy of the name Christian who cherish enmities. Hatred, dissensions and discord should be entirely put away, for in the daily sacrifice we profess nothing with more anxious care than peace and love.

It is also called "Viaticum" because it is a spiritual food which sustains us in our pilgrimage through life and paves our way to eternal glory. In accord with teaching of the Catholic Church, none of the faithful should die without this Sacrament.

The ancient Fathers, following the authority of the Apostle Paul, have sometimes called the Holy Eucharist by the name of "Supper," because it was instituted by Christ the Lord at the saving mystery of the Last Supper.

The Eucharist signifies Three Things

Catechism of the Council of Trent.

BEHOLDING the sacred mysteries with our eyes, may we also contemplate what the Sacrament of the Eucharist means.

Three things are signified in the Sacrament. The first is the Passion of Christ, something past. Our Lord himself said, "Do this as a remembrance of me," and the Apostle Paul says, "Every time you eat this bread and drink this cup, you proclaim the death of the Lord until he comes."

It also signifies divine and heavenly grace, given now in this Sacrament to nurture and preserve the soul. Just as in Baptism we are reborn to new life and by Confirmation strengthened to resist Satan and openly profess Christ's name, so by the Sacrament of the Eucharist we are nourished and supported now.

Thirdly, it is a foreshadowing of future joy and eternal glory which, in accord with God's promises, we shall receive in our heavenly home.

These three things, then, which refer clearly to past, present and future times, are so fully part of the Eucharistic mysteries that the Sacrament embraces the three as if they were one.

Litany of the Most Holy Name of Jesus

Lord, have mercy.
Christ, have mercy.
Lord, have mercy.
Jesus, hear us.
Jesus, graciously hear us.

God, the Father of Heaven, have mercy on us.*
God the Son, Redeemer of the world,
God, the Holy Spirit,
Holy Trinity, one God,
Jesus, Son of the living God,
Jesus, Splendor of the Father,
Jesus, Brightness of eternal Light,
Jesus, King of Glory,
Jesus, Sun of Justice,
Jesus, Son of the Virgin Mary,
Jesus, most amiable,
Jesus, most admirable,
Jesus, the mighty God,
Jesus, Father of the world to come,
Jesus, angel of great counsel,
Jesus, most powerful,
Jesus, most patient,
Jesus, most obedient,
Jesus, meek and humble of heart,
Jesus, lover of Chastity,
Jesus, our Lover,
Jesus, God of Peace,
Jesus, Author of Life,
Jesus, Model of Virtues,
Jesus, zealous for souls,
Jesus, our God,
Jesus, our Refuge,
Jesus, Father of the Poor,
Jesus, Treasure of the Faithful,
Jesus, good Shepherd,
Jesus, true Light,
Jesus, eternal Wisdom,

* *"Have mercy on us" is repeated after each invocation down to Jesus, Crown of all Saints.*

Jesus, infinite Goodness,
Jesus, our Way and our Life,
Jesus, joy of the Angels,
Jesus, King of Patriarchs,
Jesus, Master of the Apostles,
Jesus, Teacher of the Evangelists,
Jesus, Strength of Martyrs,
Jesus, Light of Confessors,
Jesus, Purity of Virgins,
Jesus, Crown of all Saints,
Be merciful, spare us, O Jesus!
Be merciful, graciously hear us, O Jesus!
From all evil, deliver us, O Jesus.*
From all sin,
From your wrath,
From the snares of the devil,
From the spirit of fornication,
From everlasting death,
From the neglect of your inspirations,
Through the mystery of your holy Incarnation,
Through your Nativity,
Through your Infancy,
Through your most divine Life,
Through your Labors,
Through your Agony and Passion,
Through your Cross and Dereliction,
Through your Sufferings,
Through your Death and Burial,
Through your Resurrection,
Through your Ascension,
Through your Institution of the Most Holy
   Eucharist,

* *"Deliver us, O Jesus" is repeated after each invocation down
to "Through your Glory."*

Through your Joys,

Through your Glory,

Lamb of God, who take away the sins of the world,

  spare us, O Jesus!

Lamb of God, who take away the sins of the world,

  graciously hear us, O Jesus!

Lamb of God, who take away the sins of the world,

  have mercy on us, O Jesus!

Jesus, hear us.

Jesus, graciously hear us.

THE RECEPTION OF HOLY COMMUNION OUTSIDE MASS

Believing in Jesus Christ, we should desire to receive him in Holy Communion, even when we cannot participate in the Mass. The sick and the aged especially should nourish themselves frequently on the Bread of Life.

Communion may be given outside Mass on any day and at any hour. . . . Nevertheless:

a) on Holy Thursday, communion may be given only during Mass; communion may be brought to the sick at any hour of the day;

b) on Good Friday communion may be given only during the celebration of the Passion of the Lord; communion may be brought to the sick who cannot participate in the celebration at any hour of the day;

c) on Holy Saturday, communion may be given only as viaticum.

The priest and deacon are the ministers of Holy Communion. Other special ministers too may be appointed by the bishop.

Preparations for Communion

A suitable table covered with a cloth and provided with candles should be available when communion is brought to a private home.

The Eucharist can be received under the appearance of wine by those who cannot receive the consecrated bread.

Eucharistic Fast

The sick and those of advanced age are to observe a fast from solid food and beverages, with the exception of water, for about a quarter of an hour before communion.

Other communicants should fast generally for one hour before communion.

The Communion Service

The Communion Service begins with a short penitential rite, like that at Mass.

A celebration of the Word of God may then take place, comprising one or more readings, a psalm, a period of silence and some general intercessions (see pp. 277-310).

After saying the Our Father together, the Sacrament is offered to the communicant. Presenting the Sacrament, the minister says "The Body of Christ." The communicant answers "Amen."

A short prayer and concluding rite follow.

A SAMPLE SERVICE

Antiphon

Body of Jesus, born of the Virgin Mary,
body bowed in agony,
raised upon the cross
and offered for us in sacrifice,
body pierced and flowing with blood and water,
come at the hour of our death
as our living bread,
the foretaste of eternal glory:
come, Lord Jesus,
loving and gracious Son of Mary.

Gospel   John 15:1-8

✠ A reading from the holy gospel according to
John

Jesus said to his disciples:
"I am the true vine
and my Father is the vinegrower.
He prunes away
every barren branch,
but the fruitful ones
he trims clean
to increase their yield.
You are clean already,
thanks to the word I have spoken to you.
Live on in me, as I do in you.
No more than a branch can bear fruit of itself
apart from the vine,
can you bear fruit
apart from me.

"I am the vine, you are the branches.
He who lives in me and I in him,
will produce abundantly,
for apart from me you can do nothing.
A man who does not live in me
is like a withered, rejected branch,
picked up to be thrown in the fire and burnt.
If you live in me,
and my words stay part of you,
you may ask what you will—
it will done for you.
My Father has been glorified
in your bearing much fruit
and becoming my disciples."

This is the gospel of the Lord.

Holy Communion

The minister says:

Let us pray with confidence to the Father
in the words our Savior gave us:

He continues with the people:

Our Father . . . .

The minister may invite the people in these or similar words:

Let us offer each other the sign of peace.

All make an appropriate sign of peace, according to local custom.
The minister genuflects. Taking the host, he raises it slightly over the vessel or pyx and, facing the people, says:

This is the Lamb of God
who takes away the sins of the world.
Happy are those who are called to his supper.

The communicants say once:

Lord, I am not worthy to receive you,
but only say the word and I shall be healed.

Then he takes the vessel or pyx and goes to the communicants. He takes a host for each one, raises it slightly, and says:

The body of Christ.

The communicant answers:

Amen,

and receives communion.

The minister then says the concluding prayer:

Lord,
we thank you for the nourishment you give us
through your holy gift.
Pour out your Spirit upon us
and in the strength of this food from heaven
keep us single-minded in your service.

We ask this in the name of Jesus the Lord.

The people answer: Amen.

Prayers of Thanksgiving

PRAYER TO OUR REDEEMER

Soul of Christ, make me holy.
Body of Christ, be my salvation.
Blood of Christ, let me drink your wine.
Water flowing from the side of Christ, wash me
  clean.

Passion of Christ, strengthen me.
Kind Jesus, hear my prayer;
hide me within your wounds
and keep me close to you.
Defend me from the evil enemy.

Call me at my death
to the fellowship of your saints,
that I may sing your praise with them
through all eternity. Amen.

PRAYER OF SELF-DEDICATION TO JESUS CHRIST

Lord Jesus Christ,
take all my freedom,
my memory, my understanding, and my will.
All that I have and cherish
you have given me.

I surrender it all to be guided by your will.
Your grace and your love
are wealth enough for me.
Give me these, Lord Jesus,
and I ask for nothing more.

PRAYER TO JESUS CHRIST CRUCIFIED

My good and dear Jesus,
I kneel before you,
asking you most earnestly
to engrave upon my heart
a deep and lively faith, hope, and charity,
with true repentance for my sins,
and a firm resolve to make amends.
As I reflect upon your five wounds,
and dwell upon them with deep compassion and
    grief,
I recall, good Jesus, the words the prophet David
    spoke
long ago concerning yourself:
they have pierced my hands and my feet,
they have counted all my bones!

THE UNIVERSAL PRAYER
(Attributed to Pope Clement XI)

Lord, I believe in you: increase my faith.
I trust in you: strengthen my trust.
I love you: let me love you more and more.
I am sorry for my sins: deepen my sorrow.

I worship you as my first beginning,
I long for you as my last end,
I praise you as my constant helper,
and call on you as my loving protector.

Guide me by your wisdom,
correct me with your justice,
comfort me with your mercy,
protect me with your power.

I offer you, Lord, my thoughts: to be fixed on you;
my words: to have you for their theme;
my actions: to reflect my love for you;
my sufferings: to be endured for your greater
    glory.

I want to do what you ask of me:
in the way you ask,
for 'as long as you ask,
because you ask it.

Lord, enlighten my understanding,
strengthen my will,
purify my heart,
and make me holy.

Help me to repent of my past sins
and to resist temptation in the future.
Help me to rise above my human weaknesses
and to grow stronger as a Christian.

Let me love you, my Lord and my God,
and see myself as I really am:
a pilgrim in this world,
a Christian called to respect and love
all whose lives I touch,
those in authority over me
or those under my authority,
my friends and my enemies.

Help me to conquer anger with gentleness,
greed by generosity,
apathy by fervor.
Help me to forget myself
and reach out toward others.

Make me prudent in planning,
courageous in taking risks.

Make me patient in suffering, unassuming in prosperity.

Keep me, Lord, attentive at prayer,
temperate in food and drink,
diligent in my work,
firm in my good intentions.

Let my conscience be clear,
my conduct without fault,
my speech blameless,
my life well-ordered.

Put me on guard against my human weaknesses.
Let me cherish your love for me,
keep your law,
and come at last to your salvation.

Teach me to realize that this world is passing,
that my true future is the happiness of heaven,
that life on earth is short,
and the life to come eternal.

Help me to prepare for death
with a proper fear of judgment,
but a greater trust in your goodness.
Lead me safely through death
to the endless joy of heaven.

Grant this through Christ our Lord. Amen.

NEW RITE OF PENANCE

(Extracted from the Rite of Penance approved for use in the United States beginning January 1, 1976)

TEXTS FOR THE PENITENT

The penitent should prepare for the celebration of the sacrament by prayer, reading of Scripture, and silent reflection. The penitent should think over and should regret all sins since the last celebration of the sacrament. ....

Reception of the Penitent

The penitent enters the confessional or other place set aside for the celebration of the sacrament of penance. After the welcoming of the priest, the penitent makes the sign of the cross saying:

In the name of the Father, and of the Son, and of the Holy Spirit. Amen.

The penitent is invited to have trust in God and replies:
Amen.

Reading of the Word of God

The penitent then listens to a text of Scripture which tells about God's mercy and calls man to conversion.

Confession of Sins and Acceptance of Satisfaction

The penitent speaks to the priest in a normal, conversational fashion. The penitent tells when he or she last celebrated the sacrament and then confesses his or her sins. The penitent then listens to any advice the priest may give and accepts the satisfaction from the priest. The penitent should ask any appropriate questions.

Prayer of the Penitent and Absolution

Prayer

Before the absolution is given, the penitent expresses sorrow for sins in these or similar words:

My God,
I am sorry for my sins with all my heart.
In choosing to do wrong
and failing to do good,

334

I have sinned against you
whom I should love above all things.
I firmly intend, with your help,
to do penance,
to sin no more,
and to avoid whatever leads me to sin.
Our Savior Jesus Christ
suffered and died for us.
In his name, my God, have mercy.

OR:

Remember, Lord, your compassion and mercy
   which you showed long ago.
Do not recall the sins and failings of my youth.
In your mercy remember me, Lord because of
   your goodness.

OR:

Wash me from my guilt
and cleanse me of my sin.
I acknowledge my offense;
my sin is before me always.

OR:

Father, I have sinned against you
and am not worthy to be called your son.
Be merciful to me, a sinner.

OR:

Father of mercy,
like the prodigal son
I return to you and say:
"I have sinned against you
and am no longer worthy to be called your son."
Christ Jesus, Savior of the world,
I pray with the repentant thief
to whom you promised Paradise:

"Lord, remember me in your kingdom."
Holy Spirit, fountain of love,
I call on you with trust:
"Purify my heart,
and help me to walk as a child of light."

OR:

Lord Jesus,
you opened the eyes of the blind,
healed the sick,
forgave the sinful woman,
and after Peter's denial confirmed him in your
    love.
Listen to my prayer,
forgive all my sins,
renew your love in my heart,
help me to live in perfect unity with my fellow
    Christians
that I may proclaim your saving power to all the
    world.

OR:

Lord Jesus,
you choose to be called the friend of sinners,
By your saving death and resurrection
free me from my sins.
May your peace take root in my heart
and bring forth a harvest
of love, holiness, and truth.

OR:

Lord Jesus Christ,
you are the Lamb of God;
you take away the sins of the world.
Through the grace of the Holy Spirit
restore me to friendship with your Father,

cleanse me from every stain of sin
and raise me to new life
for the glory of your name.

OR:

Lord God,
in your goodness have mercy on me:
do not look on my sins,
but take away all my guilt.
Create in me a clean heart
and renew within me an upright spirit.

OR:

Lord Jesus, Son of God,
have mercy on me, a sinner.

Absolution

If the penitent is not kneeling, he or she bows his or her head as the priest extends his hands (or at least extends his right hand).

God, the Father of mercies,
through the death and resurrection of his Son
has reconciled the world to himseelf
and sent the Holy Spirit among us
for the forgiveness of sins;
through the ministry of the Church
may God give you pardon and peace,
and I absolve you from your sins
in the name of the Father, and of the Son,
and of the Holy Spirit.
Amen.

Proclamation of Praise of God and Dismissal

Penitent and priest give praise to God.

Priest: Give thanks to the Lord, for he is good.
Penitent: His mercy endures for ever.

Then the penitent is dismissed by the priest.

FORM OF EXAMINATION OF CONSCIENCE

This suggested form for an examination of conscience should be completed and adapted to meet the needs of different individuals and to follow local usages.

In an examination of conscience, before the sacrament of penance, each individual should ask himself these questions in particular:

1. What is my attitude to the sacrament of penance? Do I sincerely want to be set free from sin, to turn again to God, to begin a new life, and to enter into a deeper friendship with God? Or do I look on it as a burden, to be undertaken as seldom as possible?

2. Did I forget to mention, or deliberately conceal, any grave sins in past confessions?

3. Did I perform the penance I was given? Did I make reparation for any injury to others? Have I tried to put into practice my resolution to lead a better life in keeping with the Gospel?

Each individual should examine his life in the light of God's word.

I. The Lord says: "You shall love the Lord your God with your whole heart."

1. Is my heart set on God, so that I really love him above all things and am faithful to his commandments, as a son loves his father? Or am I more concerned about the things of this world? Have I a right intention in what I do?

2. God spoke to us in his Son. Is my faith in God firm and secure? Am I wholehearted in accepting the Church's teaching? Have I been careful to grow in my understanding of the faith, to hear God's word, to listen to instructions on the faith, to avoid dangers to faith? Have I been

always strong and fearless in professing my faith in God and the Church? Have I been willing to be known as a Christian in private and public life?

3. Have I prayed morning and evening? When I pray, do I really raise my mind and heart to God or is it a matter of words only? Do I offer God my difficulties, my joys, and my sorrows? Do I turn to God in time of temptation?

4. Have I love and reverence for God's name? Have I offended him in blasphemy, swearing falsely, or taking his name in vain? Have I shown disrespect for the Blessed Virgin Mary and the saints?

5. Do I keep Sundays and feast days holy by taking a full part, with attention and devotion, in the liturgy, and especially in the Mass? Have I fulfilled the precept of annual confession and of communion during the Easter season?

6. Are there false gods that I worship by giving them greater attention and deeper trust than I give to God: money, superstition, spiritism, or other occult practices?

II. The Lord says: "Love one another as I have loved you."

1. Have I a genuine love for my neighbors? Or do I use them for my own ends, or do to them what I would not want done to myself? Have I given grave scandal by my words or actions?

2. In my family life, have I contributed to the well-being and happiness of the rest of the family by patience and genuine respect and giving them help in their spiritual and material needs? Have

I been careful to give a Christian upbringing to my children, and to help them by good example and by exercising authority as a parent. Have I been faithful to my husband (wife) in my heart and in my relations with others?

3. Do I share my possessions with the less fortunate? Do I do my best to help the victims of oppression, misfortune, and poverty? Or do I look down on my neighbor, especially the poor, the sick, the elderly, strangers, and people of other races?

4. Does my life reflect the mission I received in confirmation? Do I share in the apostolic and charitable works of the Church and in the life of my parish? Have I helped to meet the needs of the Church and of the world and prayed for them: for unity in the Church, for the spread of the Gospel among the nations, for peace and justice, etc.?

5. Am I concerned for the good and prosperity of the human community in which I live, or do I spend my life caring only for myself? Do I share to the best of my ability in the work of promoting justice, morality, harmony, and love in human relations? Have I done my duty as a citizen? Have I paid my taxes?

6. In my work or profession am I just, hardworking, honest, serving society out of love for others? Have I paid a fair wage to my employees? Have I been faithful to my promises and contracts?

7. Have I obeyed legitimate authority and given it due respect?

8. If am in a position of responsibility or au-

thority, do I use this for my own advantage or for the good of others, in a spirit of service?

9. Have I been truthful and fair, or have I injured others by deceit, calumny, detraction, rash judgment, or violation of a secret?

10. Have I done violence to others by damage to life or limb, reputation, honor, or material possessions? Have I involved them in loss? Have I been responsible for advising an abortion or procuring one? Have I kept up hatred for others? Am I estranged from others through quarrels, enmity, insults, anger? Have I been guilty of refusing to testify to the innocence of another because of selfishness?

11. Have I stolen the property of others? Have I desired it unjustly and inordinately? Have I damaged it? Have I made restitution of other people's property and made good their loss?

12. If I have been injured, have I been ready to make peace for the love of Christ and to forgive, or do I harbor hatred and the desire for revenge?

III. Christ our Lord says: "Be perfect as your Father is perfect."

1. Where is my life really leading me? Is the hope of eternal life my inspiration? Have I tried to grow in the life of the Spirit through prayer, reading the word of God and meditating on it, receiving the sacraments, self-denial? Have I been anxious to control vices, my bad inclinations and passions, e.g., envy, of food and drink? Have I been proud and boastful, thinking myself better in the sight of God and despising others as

less important than myself? Have I imposed my own will on others, without respecting their freedom and rights?

2. What use have I made of time, of health and strength, of the gifts God has given me to be used like the talents in the Gospel? Do I use them to become more perfect every day? Or have I been lazy and too much given to leisure?

3. Have I been patient in accepting the sorrows and disappointments of life? How have I performed mortification so as to "fill up what is wanting to the sufferings of Christ?" Have I kept the precept of fasting and abstinence?

4. Have I kept my senses and my whole body pure and chaste as a temple of the Holy Spirit consecrated for resurrection and glory, and as a sign of God's faithful love for men and women, a sign that is seen most perfectly in the sacrament of matrimony? Have I dishonored my body by fornication, impurity, unworthy conversation or thoughts, evil desires or actions? Have I given in to sensuality? Have I indulged in reading, conversation, shows, and entertainments that offend against Christian and human decency? Have I encouraged others to sin by my own failure to maintain these standards? Have I been faithful to the moral law in my married life?

5. Have I gone against my conscience out of fear or hypocrisy?

6. Have I always tried to act in the true freedom of the sons of God according to the law of the Spirit, or am I the slave of forces within me?

EVERYDAY PRAYERS

IN THE Name of the Father, and of the Son, and of the Holy Spirit. Amen.

The Lord's Prayer

OUR Father, who art in heaven,
hallowed be thy name;
thy kingdom come;
thy will be done on earth as it is in heaven.
Give us this day our daily bread;
and forgive us our trespasses
as we forgive those who trespass against us;
and lead us not into temptation,
but deliver us from evil.

The Hail Mary

HAIL, Mary, full of grace, the Lord is with you.
Blessed are you among women,
and blessed is the fruit of your womb, Jesus.
Holy Mary, Mother of God, pray for us sinners,
now and at the hour of our death. Amen.

The Doxology

GLORY to the Father, and to the Son, and to
the Holy Spirit;
as it was in the beginning, is now, and will be
for ever. Amen.

The Apostles' Creed

I BELIEVE in God, the Father almighty,
creator of heaven and earth.
I believe in Jesus Christ, his only Son, our Lord.
He was conceived by the power of the Holy
Spirit

343

and born of the Virgin Mary.
He suffered under Pontius Pilate,
    was crucified, died, and was buried.
  He descended to the dead.
  On the third day he rose again.
  He ascended into heaven,
    and is seated at the right of the Father.
  He will come again to judge the living and the
    dead.
I believe in the Holy Spirit,
  the holy catholic Church,
  the communion of saints,
  the forgiveness of sins,
  the resurrection of the body,
  and the life everlasting.

Psalm 23

THE Lord is my shepherd;
  there is nothing I shall want.
Fresh and green are the pastures
where he gives me repose.
Near restful waters he leads me,
to revive my drooping spirit.
He guides me along the right path;
he is true to his name.
If I should walk in the valley of darkness
no evil would I fear.
You are there with your crook and your staff;
with these you give me comfort.
You have prepared a banquet for me
in the sight of my foes.
My head you have anointed with oil;
my cup is overflowing.
Surely goodness and kindness shall follow me

all the days of my life.
In the Lord's own house shall I dwell
for ever and ever.

My Way of Life

GOD has created me to do him some definite
service;
He has committed some work to me which
he has not committed to another.
I have my mission . . .
I am a link in a chain, a bond of connection
between persons.
He has not created me for naught . . .
Therefore I will trust him.
Whatever, wherever I am, I can never be
thrown away . . .
He does nothing in vain, He knows what he
is about.

John Henry Newman

For Cities

CITIES are for needs and wants,
divine Father,
that cannot be met in isolation.
Have we expected from them too much
and put in too little?
Spur us to renew our cities
as you renew the earth in spring
that families may have decent living space
that the poor may have hope fulfilled
that the sick and aged
may be treated as persons.
May our cities

be filled with love
truly homes and not merely structures.
Amen.

The Christophers

For Neighbors

HELP me to understand the answer
Jesus gave to the question:
"Who is my neighbor?"
About a man on a road who needed help
about those who refused it
and the one person who gave it.
Make me more sensitive
to the feelings of those I meet
at home, in a store, on a bus, in a crowd.
More aware
that whether I know them or not —
the nameless, the angry, the anguished
all people, everywhere
are my neighbors in you.
No one is really a stranger
unless I choose to make him so. Amen.

The Christophers

To Know Myself

FATHER, help me to know myself
what I am and what I can become.
Enable me to see the good in myself
and rejoice in it
to see flaws and change them.
Teach me to live with myself,
to accept myself.
Remind me

that becoming what You want me to be
is more like cultivating a garden
than chopping down a forest.
Amen.

The Christophers

One Minute at a Time

YOU give me today, one minute at a time.
That's all I have, all I ever will have.
Give me the faith
that knows that each moment
contains exactly what is best for me.
Give me the hope
that trusts You in trials.
Give me the love that makes each minute
an anticipation of eternity with You.
Amen.

The Christophers

For Perseverance

MAY he support us all the day long,
till the shades lengthen
and the evening comes
and the busy world is hushed
and the fever of life is over
and our work is done —
then in his mercy —
may he give us a safe lodging
and a holy rest
and peace at last.

John Henry Newman

GUIDE FOR HYMNS

O Come, O Come, Emmanuel

John M. Neale, Tr.   Melody adapted by T. Helmore

O come, O come, Emmanuel,
And ransom captive Israel,
That mourns in lowly exile here,
Until the Son of God appear.

Refrain: Rejoice! Rejoice! O Israel,
To thee shall come Emmanuel.

O come thou Day-spring come and cheer
Our spirits by thine advent here!
Disperse the gloomy clouds of night
And death's dark shadows put to flight.

O come, O come, thou Lord of might,
Who to the tribes on Sinai's height
In ancient times you gave the law
In cloud and majesty and awe.

What Child Is This

What child is this, who laid to rest,
On Mary's lap is sleeping?
Whom angels greet with anthem's sweet,
While shepherds watch are keeping?

Refrain: This, this is Christ the King,
whom shepherds guard and angels sing:
Haste, haste to bring him laud,
The Babe, the Son of Mary.

Why lies he in such mean estate
Where ox and ass are feeding?
Good Christian fear, for sinner's here
The silent Word is pleading:

So bring him incense, gold, and myrrh,
Come peasant, king to own him,
The King of kings salvation brings,
Let loving hearts enthrone him.

3 Hail, Holy Queen Enthroned Above

Hail, holy Queen enthroned above, O Maria!
   Hail, Mother of mercy and of love, O Maria!

Refrain: Triumph, all ye cherubim,
            Sing with us, ye seraphim,
            Heav'n and earth resound the hymn.
          Salve, salve, salve Regina.

2. Our life, our sweetness here below, O Maria!
   Our hope in sorrow and in woe, O Maria!

          Refrain:

3. To thee we cry, poor sons of Eve, O Maria!
   To thee we sigh, we mourn, we grieve, O Maria!

          Refrain:

4. Turn, then, most gracious Advocate, O Maria!
   Toward us thine eyes compassionate, O Maria!

          Refrain:

5. When this our exile's time is o'er, O Maria!
   Show us thy Son for evermore, O Maria!

          Refrain:

Sing of Mary, Pure and Lowly

4

Trier, 1695

1. Sing of Ma - ry, pure and low - ly,
2. Sing of Je - sus; son of Ma - ry,
3. Glo - ry be to God the Fa - ther,

Vir - gin - moth - er un - de - filed,
In the home at Na - za - reth.
Glo - ry be to God the Son;

Sing of God's own Son most ho - ly,
Toil and la - bor can - not wea - ry
Glo - ry be to God the Spir - it;

Who be - came her lit - tle child.
Love en - dur - ing un - to death.
Glo - ry to the Three in One.

Fair - est child of fair - est moth - er,
Con - stant was the love he gave her,
From the heart of bless - ed Ma - ry,

God the Lord who came to earth,
Though he went forth from her side,
From all saints the song as - cends,

Word made flesh, our ve - ry broth - er,
Forth to preach, and heal, and suf - fer,
And the Church the strain re - ec - hoes

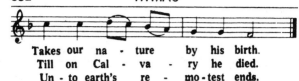

Takes our na - ture   by his birth.
Till on Cal - va - ry he died.
Un - to earth's re - mo - test ends.

5 We Three Kings

1. We three kings of Orient are
   Bearing gifts we traverse afar,
   Field and fountain, moor and mountain,
   Following yonder Star.

   Refrain: O Star of wonder, Star of night,
   Star with royal beauty bright,
   Westward leading, still proceeding,
   Guide us to thy perfect light,

2. Born a king on Bethlehem's plain,
   Gold I bring to crown Him again,
   King forever, ceasing never,
   Over us all to reign. —*Refrain*

3. Frankincense to offer have I
   Incense owns a Deity high,
   Prayer and praising, all men raising.
   Worship Him, God most High. —*Refrain*

6 Lord, Who throughout These 40 Days

1. Lord, who throughout these forty days
       For us did fast and pray,
   Teach us with you to mourn our sins,
       And close by you to stay.

2. And through these days of penitence,
       And through your Passiontide,
   Yea, evermore, in life and death,
       Jesus! with us abide.

3. Abide with us, that so, this life
       Of suff'ring over past,
   An Easter of unending joy
       We may attain at last! Amen.

Sing My Tongue the Savior's Glory   7

1. Sing my tongue, the Savior's glory,
   Of his flesh the mystr'y sing;
   Of the Blood all price exceeding,
   Shed by our immortal King,
   Destined for the world's redemption,
   From a noble womb to spring.

2. Of a pure and spotless Virgin
   Born for us on earth below,
   He, as Man, with man conversing,
   Stayed, the seeds of truth to sow;
   Then he closed in solemn order
   Wondrously his life of woe.

3. On the night of that Last Supper,
   Seated with his chosen band,
   He the Paschal victim eating,
   First fulfils the Law's command;
   Then as food to his Apostles
   Give himself with his own Hand.

4. Word made flesh the bread of nature
   By his word to Flesh he turns;
   Wine into his blood he changes
   What though sense no change discerns?
   Only he the heart in earnest,
   Faith her lesson quickly learns.

(Tantum ergo)

5. Down in adoration falling
   Lo! the sacred Host we hail
   Lo! o'er ancient forms departing,
   Newer rites of grace prevail;
   Faith for all defects supplying,
   Where the feeble senses fail.

6. To the Everlasting Father,
   And the Son who reigns on high,
   With the Holy Ghost proceeding
   Forth from each eternally
   Be salvation honor, blessing,
   Might, and endless majesty. Amen.

8

Were You There

1. Were you there when they crucified my Lord?
   Were you there when they crucified my Lord? Oh!
   Sometimes it causes me to tremble, tremble, tremble.
   Were you there when they crucified my Lord?

2. Were you there when they nailed him to the tree?
   Were you there when they nailed him to the tree? Oh!
   Sometimes it causes me to tremble, tremble, tremble.
   Were you there when they nailed him to the tree?

3. Were you there when they laid him in the tomb?
   Were you there when they laid him in the tomb? Oh!
   Sometimes it causes me to tremble, tremble, tremble.
   Were you there when they laid him in the tomb?

9

O Sacred Head Surrounded

1. O sacred Head surrounded
      By crown of piercing thorn!
   O bleeding Head, so wounded,
      Reviled, and put to scorn!
   Death's pallid hue comes ov'r you,
      The glow of life decays,
   Yet angel hosts adore you,
      And tremble as they gaze.

2. I see your strength and vigor
      All fading in the strife,
   And death with cruel rigor,
      Bereaving you of life.
   O agony and dying!
      O love to sinners free!
   Jesus, all grace supplying,
      O turn your face on me.

All Glory, Laud and Honor

Refrain:

All glory, praise, and honor
To you, Redeemer, King!
To whom the lips of children
Made glad hosannas ring.

1

You are the King of Israel,
And David's royal Son,
Who in the Lord's Name
  comes,
The King and Blessed One.
                    Refrain

2

The company of angels
Are praising you on high;
And mortal men and all
  things
Created make reply. Refrain

3

The people of the Hebrews
With palms before you went:
Our praise and prayers and
  anthems
Before you we present.
                    Refrain

4

To you before your Passion
They sang their hymns of
  praise:
To you, now high exalted,
Our melody we raise. Refrain

5

As once you did accept their
  praise,
Accept the praise we bring,
You who rejoice in ev'ry
  good,
Our good and gracious King.
                    Refrain

Jesus Christ Is Risen Today

1. Jesus Christ is ris'n today, **alleluia!**
   Our triumphant holy day, **alleluia.**
   Who did once upon the cross, **alleluia!**
   Suffer to redeem our loss, **alleluia.**

2. Hymns of praise then let us sing, **alleluia!**
   Unto Christ our heav'nly King, **alleluia!**
   Who endured the cross and grave, **alleluia.**
   Sinners to redeem and save, **alleluia!**

3. Sing we to our God above, **alleluia!**
   Praise eternal as his love, **alleluia!**
   Praise him, all ye heav'nly host, **alleluia.**
   Father, Son and Holy Ghost, **alleluia!**

12

All Hail, Adored Trinity

All hail, adored Trinity:
All hail, eternal Unity,
O God the Father, God the Son,
And God the Spirit, ever One.

2. Three Persons praise we evermore,
And One, Eternal God adore;
In thy sure mercy ever kind,
May we our true protection find.

3. O Trinity! O Unity!
Be present as we worship thee;
And with the songs the angels sing
Unite the hymns of praise we bring.

13

To Jesus Christ, Our Sovereign King

1. To Jesus Christ, our sov'reign King,
Who is the world's Salvation,
All praise and homage do we bring
And thanks and adoration.

2. Your reign extend, O King benign,
To ev'ry land and nation;
For in your kingdom, Lord divine,
Alone we find salvation.

3. To you and to your Church, great King,
We pledge our heart's oblation;
Until before your throne we sing
In endless jubilation.

Refrain:

Christ Jesus, Victor! Christ Jesus, Ruler!
Christ Jesus, Lord and Redeemer!

Come Holy Ghost, Creator Blest

14

1. Come, Holy Ghost, Creator blest,
   And in our hearts take up thy rest;
   Come with thy grace and heav'nly aid
   To fill the hearts which thou hast made,
   To fill the hearts which thou hast made.

2. O Comforter, to thee we cry,
   Thou heav'nly gift of God most high;
   Thou fount of life and fire of love
   And sweet anointing from above,
   And sweet anointing from above.

3. Praise we the Father, and the Son,
   And the blest Spirit with them one;
   And may the Son on us bestow
   The gifts that from the Spirit flow,
   The gifts that from the Spirit flow.

15

Praise My Soul, The King of Heaven

1

Praise, my soul, the King of heaven;
To his feet your tribute bring;
Ransomed, healed, restored, forgiven,
Evermore his praises sing;
Alleluia! Alleluia!

Praise him for his grace and favor
To his children in distress;
Praise him still the same as ever
Slow to chide and swift to bless:
Alleluia! Alleluia!
Glorious in his faithfulness.

3

Father-like he tends and spares us;
Well our feeble frame he knows;
In his hand he gently bears us,
Rescues us from all our foes.
Alleluia! Alleluia!
Widely yet his mercy flows.

4

Angels, help us to adore him;
You behold him face to face;
Sun and moon, howw down
Sun and moon, bow down before him,
Join the praises of our race:
Alleluia! Alleluia!
Praise with us the God of grace

16

On This Day, the First of Days

1. On this day, the first of days,
2. On this day th'e - ter - nal Son
3. Fa - ther, who didst fash - ion man
4. Word made flesh all hail to thee!
5. Ho - ly Spir - it, you im - part
6. God, the bless - ed Three in One,

1. God the Fa - ther's name we praise;
2. O - ver death his tri - umph won;
3. God - like in thy lov - ing plan,
4. Thou from sin hast set us free;
5. Gifts of love to ev - ery heart;
6. May thy ho - ly will be done;

1. Who, cre - a - tion's Lord and spring;
2. On this day the Spir - it came
3. Fill us with that love di - vine,
4. And with thee we die and rise
5. Give us light and grace, we pray,
6. In thy word our souls are free.

1. Did the world from dark - ness bring.
2. With his gifts of liv - ing flame.
3. And con - form our wills to thine.
4. Un - to God in sac - ri - fice.
5. Fill our hearts this ho - ly day.
6. And we rest this day with thee.

With Hearts Renewed

With hearts re-newed by liv - ing faith, We
So rich God's grace in Je - sus Christ, That

lift our thoughts in grate - ful prayer to
we are called as sons of light to

God our gra-cious Fa - ther. Whose plan it was to
bear the pledge of glo - ry. Through Him in Whom all

make us sons through His own Son's re-
full - ness dwells. We of - fer God our

demp - tive death that res - cued us from dark - ness.
gift of self in un - ion with the spir - it.

Lord God, Sav-ior, Gives us strength to mould our hearts in

your true life - ness. Sons and ser-vants of our Fa - ther.

18   ## Loving Shepherd of Your Sheep

1. Lov - ing Shep - herd   of   your sheep,
2. Lov - ing Shep - herd   you did give,
3. Lov - ing Shep - herd   ev - er near,

Keep   us   Lord   in   safe - ty keep;
Your   own life   that   we   might live;
Teach us   still your voice to   hear;

Noth - ing   can   your   pow'r with - stand,
May   we   love   you   day   by   day,
Suf - fer not   our   steps   to   stray

None   can   pluck us   from your hand.
Glad - ly   your sweet   Will o - bey.
From   the   straight and   nar - row way.

Good   Shep - herd,   shield   us.
Good   Shep - herd,   lead   us.
Good   Shep - herd,   guide   us.

When Morning Gilds the Skies

19

E. Caswall, Tr.   Traditional

1. When morn-ing gilds the skies My
2. Be this, while life is mine, My
3. To God, the Word, on high The
4. Let earth's wide cir-cle round In

1. heart a-wak-ing cries; May Je-sus Christ be
2. cant-i-cle di-vine; May Je-sus Christ be
3. hosts of an-gels cry; May Je-sus Christ be
4. joy-ful song re-sound; May Je-sus Christ be

1. praised! A-like at work and prayer To
2. praised! Be our e-ter-nal song, Through
3. praised! Let na-tions too up-raise Their
4. praised! Let air, and sea, and sky, Through

1. Je-sus I re-pair: May Je-sus Christ be
2. all the a-ges long. May Je-sus Christ be
3. voice in hymns of praise: May Je-sus Christ be
4. depth and height re-ply May Je-sus Christ be

1. praised! May Je-sus Christ be praised!
2. praised! May Je-sus Christ be praised!
3. praised! May Je-sus Christ be praised!
4. praised! May Je-sus Christ be praised!

20

Help Us, O Lord

W. W. Reid

J. B. Konig - W. W. Havergal

1. Help us, O Lord, to learn
2. Help us, O Lord, to live
3. Help us, O Lord, to teach

1. The truths thy Word im - parts:
2. The faith which we pro - claim,
3. The beau - ty of your ways,

1. To stud - y that thy laws may be
2. That all our thoughts and words and deeds
3. That yearn - ing souls may find the Christ,

1. In - scribed up - on our hearts.
2. May glo - ri - fy your name.
3. And sing a - loud his praise.

Text Copyright 1970, Hymn Society of America

21

God Father Praise and Glory

1. God Father, praise and glory
   Thy children bring to thee.
   Good will and peace to mankind
   Shall now forever be.

Refrain:

O most holy Trinity, Undivided Unity;
Holy God, Mighty God, God Immortal, be adored.

2. And thou, Lord Coeternal,
   God's sole begotten Son;
 O Jesus, King anointed,
   Who hast redemption won. *Refrain*

3. O Holy Ghost, Creator,
   Thou gift of God most high;
 Life, love and sacred Unction
   Our weakness thou supply. *Refrain*

Holy, Holy, Holy   **22**

1. Holy, holy, holy! Lord God almighty.
   Early in the morning our song shall rise to thee:
   Holy, holy, holy! Merciful and mighty,
   God in three persons, blessed Trinity.

2. Holy, holy, holy! Lord God almighty.
   All thy works shall praise thy name in earth and
     sky and sea;
   Holy, holy, holy! Merciful and mighty,
   God in three persons, blessed Trinity.

O God, Our Help in Ages Past   **23**

1.
O God, our help in ages past,
  Our hope for years to
    come,
Our shelter from the stormy
  blast,
  And our eternal home.

2.
Under the shadow of Thy
  throne,
  Thy saints have dwelt
    secure.
Sufficient is Thine arm
  alone,
  And our defense is sure.

3.
A thousand ages in Thy
  sight,
  Are like an evening gone:
Short as the watch that
  ends the night,
  Before the rising sun.

4.
O God, our help in ages past,
  Our hope for years to
    come,
Be Thou our guide while
  troubles last,
  And our eternal home.
                                    I. Watts.

24 ## Now Thank We All Our God

1. Now thank we all our God,
   With heart and hands and voices,
   Who wondrous things hath done,
   In whom his world rejoices;
   Who from our mother's arms
   Hath blessed us on our way
   With countless gifts of love,
   And still is ours today.

2. All praise and thanks to God,
   The Father now be given,
   The Son, and him who reigns
   With them in highest heaven,
   The one eternal God
   Whom earth and heav'n adore;
   For thus it was, is now,
   And shall be ever more.

25

Praise the Lord, Ye Heavens, Adore Him

1. Praise the Lord, ye heavens, adore him;
   Praise him, angels in the height;
   Sun and moon, rejoice before him;
   Praise him, all ye stars of light.
   Praise the Lord for he has spoken;
   Worlds his mighty voice obeyed;
   Laws which never shall be broken,
   For their guidance he has made.

2. Praise the Lord, for he is glorious,
   Never shall his promise fail;
   God has made his saints victorious,
   Sin and death shall not prevail.
   Praise the God of our salvation;
   Hosts on high his power proclaim;
   Heaven and earth and all creation,
   Praise and magnify his name.

3. Worship, honor, glory, blessing,
    Lord, we offer unto thee;
    Young and old, thy praise expressing,
    In glad homage bend the knee;
    All the saints in heaven adore thee,
    We would bow before thy throne;
    As thine angels serve before thee,
    So on earth thy will be done.

26

Let All Things Now Living

Melody: The Ash Grove
6.6.11.6.6.11.D

Music: Traditional Welsh Melody
Text: Anon.

1. Let all things now living a song of thanksgiving
    To God our Creator triumphantly raise;
    Who fashioned and made us, protected and stayed us,
    Who guideth us on to the end of our days.
    His banners are o'er us, his light goes before us,
    A pillar of fire shining forth in the night:
    Till shadows have vanished and darkness is banished,
    As forward we travel from light into Light.

2. His law he enforces, the stars in their courses,
    The sun in his orbit obediently shine,
    The hills and the mountains, the rivers and fountains,
    The depths of the ocean proclaim him divine.
    We, too, should be voicing our love and rejoicing
    With glad adoration, a song let us raise:
    Till all things now living unite in thanksgiving,
    To God in the highest, hosanna and praise.

Canticle of the Lamb

Rev. 19:1-7   s.m.s.

V. 1A Sal - va - tion, glo - ry, and pow - er to our God.
Respone I

V. 1B His judg - ments are hon - est and true.
Response II

V. 2A Sing praise to our God, all you his ser - vants.
Response I

V. 2B All who wor - ship Him rev - er - ent ly, great and small
Response II

V. 3A The Lord our all - pow - er - ful God is King.
Response I

V. 3B Let us re - joice, sing praise, and give him glo - ry.
Response II

V. 4A The wed - ding feast of the Lamb has be - gun.
Response I

V. 4B And his bride has pre - pared to wel - come him.
Response II

Response I   Response II

Al - le - lu - ia   Al - le - lu - ia   Al - le - lu - ia

Salvation, Glory

Antiphon

S.M. Skelly, S.C.

Praise   our   God,   all   you   his   ser - vants.

Verses

1. Salvation, glory and   might   belong to our God,
2. Praise   our   God,   all you his servants,
3. The Lord is   King,   our God, the Almighty,
4. For   this   is the wedding day of the Lamb,
5. She   has been   given   a dress to wear,

1. Al - le - lu - ia!   For his   judgements
2. Al - le - lu - ia!   The small and the   great, who
3. Al - le - lu - ia!   Let us rejoice and be   glad and give
4. Al - le - lu - ia!   His bride has pre   pared herself
5. Al - le - lu - ia!   Made of finest   linen,

1. are   true   and   just.
2.   re   vere him.
3.   him   glory.
4. for   the   wedding.
5. bril   liant   white.

Canticle of Mary

Lk 1:46-55

S.M. Skelly, S.C., 1975.

1. My soul proclaims the
2. From this day all generations shall

1. greatness of the Lord, my spirit re -
2. call me Blessed: the Almighty has

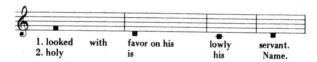

1. joices in God my Savior for he has
2. done great things for me, and

1. looked with favor on his lowly servant.
2. holy is his Name.

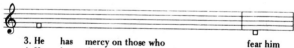

3. He has mercy on those who fear him
4. He has shown the strength of his arm,
5. He has cast down the mighty from their thrones,
6. He has filled the hungry with good things.

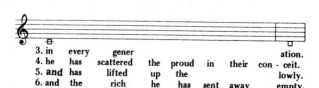

3. in every gener ation.
4. he has scattered the proud in their con - ceit.
5. and has lifted up the lowly.
6. and the rich he has sent away empty.

7. He has come to the help of his ser-vant Israel

7. for he has re - membered his promise of mercy,
   the promise he made to our fathers,

7. To Abraham and his children for - ever.

8. Glory to the Father, and to the Son,
9. As it was in the beginning, is now, and will be for ever,

8. And to the Holy Spirit,
9. A - men.

Canticle of Zechariah

1. Blessed be the Lord, the God ——— of Israel;
2. He has raised up for us a might - y savior
3. Through his holy prophets he promised of old
4. He promised to show mercy to ——— our fathers
5. This was the oath he swore to our fa - ther Abraham
6. Free to worship him with - out fear
7. You my child, shall be called the prophet of the Most High
8. To give his people knowledge of ——— sal - vation
9. In the tender compassion of ——— our God
10. To shine on those who dwell in darkness and the shadow of death
11. Glory be to the Father, and to ——— the Son,
12. As it was in the ————————— be - ginning

1. he has come to his ——— people and
2. born of the ——————— house of his
3. that he would save us from our enemies, from the hands of
4. and to re - member his
5. to set us ——————— free from the hands
6. holy and righteous in his —— sight all the days
7. for you will go before the —— Lord to pre -
8. by the for - giveness
9. the dawn from on ———— high
10. and to guide our ———— feet into the
11. and to ——————— the
12. is now, and ——————— will

1.	set	them	free.
2.	ser - vant	David.
3.	all	who	hate us;
4.	ho - ly	covenant.
5.	of	our	enemies.
6.	of	our	life.
7.	pare	his	way.
8.	of	their	sins.
9.	break	up	on us.
10.	way	of	peace.
11.	Ho - ly	Spirit:
12.	be	for - ever. Amen.

CANTICLE OF MARY ANTIPHONS

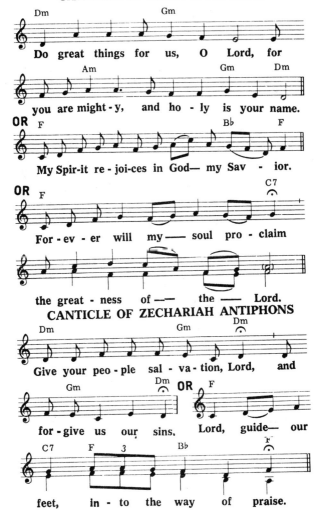

Do great things for us, O Lord, for
you are might - y, and ho - ly is your name.

OR

My Spir-it re - joi-ces in God— my Sav - ior.

OR

For - ev - er will my — soul pro - claim
the great - ness of — the — Lord.

CANTICLE OF ZECHARIAH ANTIPHONS

Give your peo - ple sal - va - tion, Lord, and
for - give us our sins. **OR** Lord, guide— our
feet, in - to the way of praise.

PRAYERS FOR TIMES OF SICKNESS AND TROUBLE

THE WISDOM OF SUFFERING

"WE HAVE the only truth capable of answering the mystery of suffering and of bringing you relief without illusion, and that is Faith and union with the Man of Sorrows, with Christ the Son of God, nailed to the Cross for our sins and for our salvation. Christ did not do away with suffering. He did not even wish to unveil to us entirely the mystery of suffering. He took it upon Himself and this is enough to make you understand its value. All of you who feel heavily the weight of the cross, you who are poor and abandoned, you who weep, you who are persecuted for justice, you who are ignored, you the unknown victims of suffering, take courage.

"You are the preferred children of the kingdom of God, the kingdom of hope, happiness and life. You are the brothers of the suffering Christ, and with Him if you wish, you are saving the world.

"This is the Christian science of suffering, the only one which gives peace. Know that you are not alone, separated, abandoned, or useless. You have been called by Christ and are His living and transparent image."

Vatican Council II, AAS, 58, 1966, 16-17

OUR Lord Jesus Christ told his followers that he was close to the sick and suffering: "I was sick and you visited me."

You are not separated from hope, or abandoned, or useless in your sickness. By faith you are united to Christ; by love he is united to you. In your sickness you feel the weight of his cross. But don't be afraid, Christ is with you. He is strong and gives life.

PRAYER FOR STRENGTH

LISTEN to me, Lord, and answer me,
  Poor and needy as I am;
Keep my soul: I am devoted to you,
  Save your servant who relies on you.
You are my God, take pity on me, Lord,
  I call you all the day long;
Give your servant reason to rejoice,
  For to you Lord, I lift up my soul.
Lord, you are good and forgiving,
  Most loving to all who call you;
Lord hear my prayer, listen to me as I plead.
Lord, teach me your way,
  How to walk beside you faithfully.
Make me single-hearted in fearing your name.
Lord God, you who are always merciful and
  Tender-hearted, slow to anger, always loving,
  Always loyal, turn to me and pity me.

Give me your strength, your saving help, me
   Your servant, give me one more proof of
   Your goodness.   **Psalm 86**

THE WORD OF THE LORD
For Times of Fear and Distress

Be firm and steadfast! Do not fear nor be dismayed, for the Lord, your God, is with you wherever you go.   **(Joshua 1:9)**

✦   ✦   ✦

The Lord is my shepherd; I shall not want. . . . I fear no evil; for you are at my side. **(Psalm 23)**

✦   ✦   ✦

The Lord is my light and my salvation; whom should I fear? The Lord is my life's refuge; of whom should I be afraid?   **(Psalm 27)**

✦   ✦   ✦

God is our refuge and our strength, an ever present help in distress. . . . The Lord of hosts is with us; our stronghold is the God of Jacob.
                            (Psalm 46)

✦   ✦   ✦

Bless the Lord, O my soul; and all my being, bless his holy name. Bless the Lord, O my soul, and forget not all his benefits; He pardons all your iniquities, he heals all your ills. **(Psalm 103)**

✦   ✦   ✦

They that hope in the Lord will renew their strength, they will soar as with eagles' wings; they will run and not grow weary, walk and not grow faint.   **(Isaiah 40:31)**

✦   ✦   ✦

They carried to him all those afflicted with various diseases and racked with pain: the possessed, the lunatics, the paralyzed. He cured them all. (Matthew 4:24)

Come to me all you who are weary and find life burdensome, and I will refresh you. (Matthew 11:28)

I assure you, unless you change and become like little children, you will not enter the kingdom of God. (Matthew 18:3)

Know that I am with you always, until the end of the world. (Matthew 28:20)

Daughter, it is your faith that has cured you. Go in peace and be free of this illness. (Mk 5:34)

I give you my word, if you are ready to believe that you will receive whatever you ask for in prayer, it shall be done for you. (Mark 11:24)

I myself am the living bread come down from heaven. If anyone eats this bread he shall live forever; the bread I will give is my flesh, for the life of the world. (John 6:51)

I am the light of the world. No follower of mine shall ever walk in darkness; no, he shall possess the light of life. (John 8:12)

The thief comes only to steal and slaughter and destroy, I came that they might have life and have it to the full.   (John 10:10)

✓   ✓   ✓

I am the resurrection and the life: whoever believes in me, though he should die, will come to life, and whoever is alive and believes in me will never die.   (John 11:25, 26)

✓   ✓   ✓

Do not let your hearts be troubled. Have faith in God and faith in me.   (John 14:1)

✓   ✓   ✓

I am the way, the truth and the life; no one comes to the Father but through me. (John 14:6)

✓   ✓   ✓

Anything you ask me in my name I will do.
          (John 14:14)

✓   ✓   ✓

Peace is my farewell to you, my peace is my gift to you; I do not give it to you as the world gives peace. Do not be distressed or fearful.
          (John 14:27)

✓   ✓   ✓

I am the vine, you are the branches. He who lives in me and I in him, will produce abundantly, for apart from me you can do nothing. Live on in me, as I do in you. No more than a branch can bear fruit of itself apart from the vine, can you bear fruit apart from me.   (John 15:5, 4)

✓   ✓   ✓

Rejoice in hope, be patient under trial, persevere in prayer. (Romans 12:12)

✓ ✓ ✓

You, then, are the body of Christ. Every one of you is a member of it. (1 Corinthians 12:27)

✓ ✓ ✓

'My grace is enough for you, for in weakness power reaches perfection.' and so I willingly boast of my weaknesses instead, that the power of Christ may rest upon me. (2 Corinthians 12:9)

✓ ✓ ✓

I wish to know Christ and the power flowing from his resurrection; likewise to know how to share in his sufferings by being formed into the pattern of his death. (Philippians 3:10)

✓ ✓ ✓

Rejoice in the Lord always! I say it again. Rejoice! (Philippians 3:10)

✓ ✓ ✓

In him who is the source of my strength I have strength for everything. (Philippians 4:13)

✓ ✓ ✓

Christ's peace must reign in your hearts, since as members of the one body you have been called to that peace. Dedicate yourselves to thankfulness. (Colossians 3:15)

✓ ✓ ✓

Here I stand, knocking at the door. If anyone hears me calling and opens the door, I will enter his house and have supper with him, and he with me. (Revelation 3:20)

✓ ✓ ✓

"Yes, I am coming soon!" Amen! Come, Lord
Jesus!   (Revelations 22:20, 21)

✓   ✓   ✓

PRAYER FOR FIDELITY IN TRIAL

LORD Jesus Christ,
    you hear the voices of the poor and the
  needy,
because by your suffering and death,
you are united to those who are afflicted.
Relieve the burden of my waiting,
for the days are long.
Take away my fears of uselessness,
keep me from discouragement,
and make me obedient to your holy will.
Then faithful to your ways
I shall feel the refreshment of your goodness,
that comes to those who seek you. Amen.

✓   ✓   ✓

PRAYER TO GOD, THE SOURCE OF HEALTH

GOD our Father, source of all health,
    Be near those who suffer in their time of
  weakness and pain;
Relieve them of their burden and heal them,
if it be your will.
Give peaceful sleep to those who need rest
for soul and body,
and be with them in their hours of silence.
Bless those who know not what another day will
  bring;

Make them ready for whatever it may be.
Whether they must stand, or sit, or stay still,
Grant them a strong spirit.

Inspire with your love those who bring
healing and care to the suffering.
May they bestow your gifts of health and strength
wherever they go.
Grant this prayer, through Christ our Lord.
Amen.

PRAYER IN TIME OF DARKNESS

OUT of the depths I cry to you,
  Lord, hear my voice . . . (Ps 130).

From my fears, failures and sins,
    I cry to you.
  Lord, hear my voice.

From the depths of my heart
    I cry to you,
  from the darkness of myself.
From life's shadows I cry to you,
  Lord, hear my voice.

For you are merciful, Lord,
  forgiving to us all.
And so I wait, Lord,
  your mercy comes
as sure as the dawn.

PRAYER TO JESUS CRUCIFIED

LORD Jesus Christ,
I thank you, who laid down your life for me
so meekly.
You bore the nails so patiently,
you were raised upon the cross so mercifully,
you hung there so painfully,
you wept so bitterly,
you cried aloud piercingly,
you shed your blood plentifully,
and for me, a sinner, you suffered death un-
questionably.

Now, Lord Jesus Christ,
I commend myself to your love,
to the power of your passion,
to the depths of your endless mercy.

Jesus Christ,
in your immeasurable pity,
keep alive within me the memory
of your bitter death,
of your holy wounds,
so that in sickness and in health,
I may remember your mercy.

Gentle Jesus,
defend me from all danger,
and keep me so that I may stand before you
in joy.
Defend my soul, Lord Jesus Christ,
which you have bought with your precious blood.
Amen.

PRAYER TO OUR MOTHER OF SORROWS

O Mother of Sorrows,
with strength from above
you stood by the cross of your Son
to share in his sufferings,
and with tender care
you bore him in your arms
mourning and weeping.

We praise you for your faith,
which accepted God's will.
We praise your hope,
which trusted God's promise.
We praise your love,
for offering yourself
in union with your Son.

Holy Mary,
may we follow your example
and stand by all your children
who need comfort and love.

Mother of God,
stand by us in our trials
and care for us in our many needs.
Pray for us now
and at the hour of our death.

Amen.

PRAYER FOR A MERCIFUL JUDGMENT

WE ADORE you, O Christ, and we bless you
—because by your holy Cross you have
deemed the world.

O Lord Jesus Christ, Son of the living God,
we pray that you place your Passion,

your Cross and holy Death,
between your judgment and our souls,
now and at the hour of our death.

Grant to the living mercy and grace,
to the dead pardon and rest,
to the church unity and peace,
and to us sinners everlasting life,
for you live and reign
with the Father and the Holy Spirit,
one God, for ever and ever. Amen.

PRAYER BEFORE THE CROSS

LORD, by your great and saving Sign,
bless this listless soul of mine.

Jesus, by your wounded feet,
   guide my path aright.
Jesus, by your nailed hands,
   move my hands to deeds of love.
Jesus, by your pierced side,
   cleanse my thoughts and desires.
Jesus, by your crown of thorns,
   subdue my pride.
Jesus, by your silence,
   still my complaints.
Jesus, by your parched lips,
   bless the words I speak.
Jesus, by your closing eyes,
   look on my sins no more.
Jesus, by your broken heart,
   draw my heart to you.

Yes, by this great and saving Sign,
   grant peace, Lord, to this soul of mine.